YOU'LL BOUNCE RIGHT BACK

THE MOTHERHOOD MYTHS THAT FAIL US AND THE TOOLS WE NEED INSTEAD

YOU'LL BOUNCE RIGHT BACK

THE MOTHERHOOD MYTHS THAT FAIL US AND THE TOOLS WE NEED INSTEAD

ANDREA SUMARA KNOX

MANUSCRIPTS
PRESS

YOU'LL BOUNCE RIGHT BACK
The Motherhood Myths That Fail Us and the Tools We Need Instead

ISBN 979-8-88926-532-0 *Paperback*

979-8-88926-533-7 *Digital Ebook*

*To my two amazing kids, who show me
every day the person I want to be.*

I'm so lucky I get to be your mom.

CONTENTS

INTRODUCTION

I love being a mom. I have two delightful kids, and watching them do what lights them up, reading bedtime stories, writing lunchbox notes, and comforting them are the greatest privileges of my life.

But this is only *part* of my motherhood story, what you might hear exchanged between acquaintances or posted on social media. I'm going to share *whole* stories with you in this book, including the parts you'd see if you cracked open a private diary or eavesdropped on an intimate conversation between close friends. I listened to many of these stories in my psychotherapy office over the past decade, where I supported pregnant and postpartum women and couples in the transition to parenthood.

I'm eager to show you the full picture of becoming a mother because I want you to be fully prepared to thrive. Motherhood is a wonderful and special journey, but there are also hard parts. If we share only the positive side, women are left unaware and unprepared. New moms are then shocked by the reality, scrambling for resources, and ashamed for having the "wrong" experience. Precious energy is diverted away from healing, bonding with baby, adjusting to this new phase of life, and *enjoying* it.

I know this from experience. Before having a baby, I relied primarily on what I observed and absorbed around me to develop my concept of motherhood. The story I heard was motherhood is natural, beautiful, and blissful, so this is where I set my expectation. Then, when my first child was born, my ideals about motherhood came crashing down. If you peeked in my window at my lowest point as a new mom, here's the moment:

I was seated in a rocking chair nursing my nine-week-old son in the woodland-themed room we carefully created for our baby. Around me, all the diapers, crib sheets, and clean clothes we would need were neatly stacked and stowed. Everything appeared in order. My husband sat in a chair opposite me, keeping me company. On this cloudy November morning, I looked out the window at the sky, feeling like I was about to break apart. Tears stung my eyes.

"I don't want to do this anymore," I said.

"Do what? Breastfeeding?" my husband asked. He leaned forward.

"No." I choked on my tears, so ashamed and deflated. "Any of it. I don't want to be a mom anymore."

Whoa. My husband and I were both shocked and confused by these feelings. This was not what we expected. We wanted this baby so much, even working through infertility. I thought it would be so fun to settle in and take care of this sweet child. But I felt absolutely trapped and overwhelmed once our baby arrived. Why wasn't I loving this like I thought I would? Why didn't I know what it would really be like?

THE REALITY OF MOTHERHOOD

It turns out I wasn't alone in misreading motherhood.

As I asked friends, witnessed the stories of my clients, and researched, I discovered women have been consistently presented with a glossy version of motherhood for generations. Today, images of beautifully perfect mothers can be found in every corner of social media. Before that, mass media outlets such as news networks and TV shows pushed the idea of mothers being happy, perfect, and seamlessly "doing it all." Walking to the grocery store checkout in the '90s meant facing a gauntlet of magazine covers touting the miracle of motherhood and featuring photos of "sexy" celebrity mothers.

What doesn't show up is transparency and education about the day-to-day life of a mother: the demands, the difficulties, and how women are transformed by the role of motherhood and expected to manage it all on our own. Much of the preparation for motherhood stops short at birth or is baby focused rather than including parents.

Inequities and infrastructure problems are still very real for mothers. Barriers like lack of standardized paid time off after the birth of a child. A "motherhood penalty" that reduces pay by 4 percent per kid (Budig 2014, 9–23). Childcare in short supply and so costly it is unaffordable for many families. Moms spending more hours each day on caregiving and household labor than men (Fry, Aragao, Hurst, and Parker 2023, 3–6). But make it sexy, because the most valued female trait in America is physical attractiveness (Parker, Horowitz, and Stepler 2017, 19–20).

Can you see how this stacks up for moms? Susan J. Douglas wrote in her book *Enlightened Sexism* women are told, "Of course you can be anything you want," but also, "Hold on, girls, only up to a certain point, and not in any way that discomfits men or pushes feminist goals one more centimeter forward" (2010, 10).

The current system expects perfection but sets us up to fail. The narrative of motherhood bliss makes room for only one outcome, stigmatizing anything else. Becoming a mother under these circumstances, lacking real information and support, increases the likelihood of a difficult transition to parenthood. Currently, as many as one in five women will have postpartum depression (Wang et al. 2021, 1). Information, support, and preparation up front are key to dialing this statistic down and families recognizing when and how to engage help.

Unfortunately, no one will give you a heads up about this in a greeting card at your baby shower or provide it in an informative pamphlet at an OBGYN visit. Most mothers don't get an accurate picture of what motherhood looks like until it hits them.

BREAKING THE SILENCE

Why aren't we acknowledging, talking about, and supporting mothers in the real experience of motherhood?

Meaningful, proactive change requires resources, vulnerability, and facing uncomfortable feelings. It calls for valuing women, reevaluating gender roles, and creating social and policy shifts. It also disrupts a dominant system that's working… for some.

A change to the existing system is a tall order, yet I believe we are ready.

Mothers deserve accurate information and robust preparation for the transition to parenthood, and that is the purpose of this book.

The experience of having my first child kicked off a mission in my life to support mothers and families that led to specialized education in perinatal issues and postpartum adjustment. I became a postpartum educator, a maternal mental health hotline volunteer, and made perinatal issues the focus of my psychotherapy practice. I've seen wonderful gains in supporting mothers and families in recent years. But so much of the work is reactive to the existing problems, and not getting out in front of them.

I want mothers to arrive at the threshold of parenthood equipped with tools and knowledge so they can be fully present and prepared for the experience once they walk through that door. Setting expectations closely aligned with the real experience of motherhood can give women a chance to flow into parenthood with more confidence, wisdom, and internal and external resources. We can take charge of this in our own homes and hearts and maybe someday flip the script on the broader social stories.

HOW TO USE THIS BOOK

In this book, I will break down ten motherhood myths and equip you with tools, resources, and a realistic mindset for becoming a mother. You will find:

1. Accurate and research-based information about the transition to motherhood;
2. Tools to carry forward and ease the challenges of the journey;
   and
3. Exercises to guide you through this life transition in your own unique way.

I'll share parts of my own story, insights from my clinical work, and interviews with perinatal experts. You'll find in-depth interviews with real mothers and hear the voices of 120 diverse moms who responded to my "Real-World Motherhood Survey" across the US. This was an open response questionnaire I started in my own community and eventually traveled around the country via social media, thanks to friends, family, and strangers.

This book is intended for expectant mothers or women in their first year of motherhood. But it is also for the people surrounding mothers: partners, providers, friends, and family who will benefit from better understanding motherhood and the process of adjustment to becoming a parent. Seasoned mothers may find this a healing resource that validates their early experience.

The use of the terms "mom" and "motherhood" refer to anyone born as a woman, identifying as a woman, or identifies with the role of "mother." This book is for all mothers, whether through childbirth, adoption, or surrogacy. There is relevance for single, married, or unmarried mothers and those in opposite- or same-sex relationships.

Each chapter explores a Motherhood Myth—common perceptions that are untrue and box us into feeling like we are failing if it doesn't match our experience. There is also a Reframe in each chapter, an alternative to the Motherhood Myth backed by data and stories. Exercises for reframing are at the end of each chapter to experiment with new tools as well as takeaways that summarize key points for easy reference. The final chapter reviews the core skills for authentic motherhood as a reminder of the wisdom collected along the way. At the end of the book, the "Postpartum Support Checklist" provides pages to gather all your resources in one place.

As you read, you will gather a powerful set of skills for your motherhood journey. While each chapter has something to offer, you can also skip right to what interests you the most. I will reinforce this early and often: Becoming a mother is your unique journey, and you decide where to direct your energy and focus.

Please note the information in this book is not meant as medical advice or mental health treatment. The resources section at the back of the book can help connect you with support if needed. Some details in stories from my clinical work and interviews have been changed or combined to maintain confidentiality.

LET'S BEGIN THE JOURNEY

Reading this introduction may feel like a lot. You might be overwhelmed, activated, excited, or skeptical, and all of that is okay. In this book, we will break it down and build you up.

You deserve the skills for a thriving transition to parenthood. Keep reading, and you will find the pitfalls to avoid, skills to embrace, and an opportunity to lean into motherhood with wisdom. You've got this, and we can be in it together.

MOTHERHOOD MYTH #1:

YOU'RE THE SAME, JUST A MOM

Pregnant with my first child, I envisioned motherhood as an extension of a life where I could plan, predict, and largely be in control. I would be the same me, just with a baby. Diaper changes, feedings, and cuddles would fall neatly into place.

But when my baby arrived, life felt completely dismantled. The baby's needs became central. Planning went out the window. The things I usually did, that I thought identified me, slipped out of reach. Surprised and uncertain how to reassemble myself, a reckoning with my identity set in.

I heard similar stories of identity change in my psychotherapy practice. Moms who responded to the Real-World Motherhood Survey said this about identity in the transition to motherhood:

> *"A completely cataclysmic shift from a person free to do what I pleased (see friends, go out, work when I need to) to a person who was very much tied to the house and struggled to do a fraction of what I did in my former life."*
>
> —*BETSY C.*

"My time and my body were no longer my own. It was a big adjustment."

—MICHELE

"I faded into the background."

—ANONYMOUS, KANSAS

"It hit me like a ton of bricks that first week that my old life, the 'me' I knew until that point, was gone forever."

—MONICA H.

"Lost who I was. No time for interests (reading, exercise). Went from a great employee at work to an average one to spend more time with family."

—ANONYMOUS, SAN DIEGO, CALIFORNIA

When I asked how prepared women felt on a scale of one to ten for what motherhood is *really* like (one: completely unprepared, ten: extremely prepared), over 75 percent responded with a rating of five or below. Just three out of 120 respondents reported a rating of nine or ten.

Clearly there is a disconnect between our expectations of motherhood and the lived experience. No wonder, because the significance of the transition to parenthood is not often talked about. We gear up for birth and baby, but preparing *ourselves* for a life transition is a missing and critical piece.

Becoming a mother is a complex process. It is not just moving from the tasks of pregnancy to birth (or surrogacy or adoption) to taking care of a baby. It even has its own word: matrescence, first offered by anthropologist Dana Raphael, PhD, and more recently revived by authors, psychologists, doctors, and others to give a fuller picture of the experience of becoming a mother (1973, 19).

Aurélie Athan, PhD, a clinical psychologist and professor of reproductive psychology at Columbia University, expands on the definition of matrescence:

- It is a developmental passage, similar to adolescence.
- Varies in length from mother to mother and may last a lifetime.
- Recurs with each child.
- Can create change in many aspects of a mother's life including biological, psychological, social, political, and spiritual realms (2023).

The framework of a developmental process gives permission to claim time, space, and compassion for the transition. If we liken it to adolescence, it may be easier to include room for trying out different ways of being, making mistakes, having "phases" we outgrow or decide don't suit us, and sometimes even feeling defiant or wanting to run away from home.

Our transition to parenthood is multidimensional and can simultaneously be difficult, stressful, growth producing, and enlightening. It will involve losses of former aspects of ourselves and our lives, and there will also be gains—sometimes delightful and unexpected ones. If we understand becoming a mother as a process, we are liberated from feeling like there is something wrong with us for experiencing the grief, loss, and gravity of the transformation.

THE REFRAME: IT'S A PROCESS

Becoming a mother is a multi-dimensional process of transformation: matrescence. You are the guide for where this transition takes you and who you ultimately become.

SUZANNE'S STORY

I interviewed my friend Suzanne about her story of identity shift as she became a mother. Suzanne has gorgeous red hair and a personality like a warm hug, and she is a sharply intelligent mother of seven children. I figured if someone knows about motherhood, she's a good bet.

Suzanne was always achievement-oriented, culminating in attending law school at Stanford. Following her law degree, she secured a clerkship with the competitive United States Courts for the Ninth Circuit and set her sights on a high-profile career in politics.

When Suzanne had her first child, she recalled, "There's an identity bit to it I wasn't prepared for at all. It unlocked something in me I guess I didn't really know was there because I'd spent my entire teenage and adult years achieving." She could be silly, sing, dance, and not have to worry about how she was perceived. "Changing diapers and feeding and playing and smiling and doing these things with my child… I had never felt more competent in anything. It was really like a switch in self-perception for me."

She faced a choice in the transition to parenthood: *Am I going to lean into this identity that differs from what I thought? Or am I going to hold on rigidly to who I thought I was before?* "I chose congruence," she said, embracing the part of herself that loved being with her child. "It was the beginning of redefining what success and happiness looks like for me. I had spent so long trying to be what other people thought I should be, and motherhood gave me some freedom to explore really being myself."

Alongside this identity process, Suzanne also described deep feelings of loss. "I just felt like there's no going back, and I think this isn't very talked about… how parenting changes you and limits you." As a new mom, she missed simple things like the freedom to go to Target. This grated against her sense of who she was. "It just felt like a pit and felt very sad, and I don't know when it went away. But even now sometimes I'm like, what would a different life look like?" Being a mother turned out to be something beautiful for her, *and* it wasn't without grief.

To me, Suzanne's story is so whole. There is beauty, hardship, and tough decisions. It wasn't a straightforward or seamless process. Your experience of motherhood may look different from Suzanne's, but there are gems we can carry forward from her story.

- Matrescence may present new facets of your identity, and you can choose what congruence looks like for you and where to lean in. It's an opportunity for redefining.

- You may be faced with letting go of parts of your identity or your life that feel surprising. A sense of relief, joy, loss, grief, confusion, sadness, and anger are all normal feelings.

ADDITIONAL PERSPECTIVES

Becoming a mother is a transition that will intersect with your identity, in ways individual to you. Here are additional perspectives of matrescence:

"I felt completely at sea as a mom. It didn't feel like my identity at all. I often tell people that my very best day of parenting was the day I went back to work because I got to reconnect with the part of me that I was competent in."

—ALICE A.

"I chose to shift to part time work to be home more for child-care, which was something I never thought I'd want to do and still question. I think my idea of motherhood before children was that the baby would slip right into the life I had already created for myself, and the reality is that life no longer exists. It's a challenging mix of mourning the independence and actually wanting to spend all my time with my baby."

—ANONYMOUS, MASSACHUSETTS

KNOWING WHAT TO EXPECT

Your transition to becoming a mother will be uniquely yours, but understanding how it may look can help you tune in to the process and what you need in response. Here are the range of experiences surrounding identity during matrescence, shared by women in my therapy office:

- A sense of loss and grief
- Changes in priorities and values
- Less discretionary time for activities tied to identity
- A sense of confinement/lack of freedom
- Shifts in social relationships
- Less availability or capacity to work, real or perceived by self
- Less availability or capacity to work, real or perceived by the workplace
- More or less interest in working
- Shift in available energy
- Hyper-focus on baby
- Confusion or lack of self-identity
- Changes in identity expressed through body/physical appearance
- Expansion of a sense of love
- A new sense of meaning
- Proficiency in new skills

In your journey, you may experience a few of these or check off the whole list. Maybe none of these will be an exact fit for you. They may feel temporary or permanent. You won't know exactly how it will all unfold until it happens, and you don't need to. The point is to develop a sense of the possible change. When we are able to acknowledge and name what we are experiencing, we can struggle less against our feelings and better identify our needs.

CURIOSITY, SPACE, AND GRACE

What to do with all these shifts and changes? Get curious and notice them. Give yourself space to reflect on your process. And give yourself grace to be in it and be a little messy, letting go of the idea you need to do it a certain way. The way *you* find through it will be right for you.

. . . .

EXERCISES FOR REFRAMING

. . . .

CHECK IN WITH YOUR PROCESS

Create space for acknowledging matrescence through checking in with yourself. Below are questions for your reflection you can explore at any time in your process of matrescence, including before baby arrives.

WAYS TO WORK IT IN

Keep a journal during pregnancy to note your answers over time. Ask a friend to be a safe space to discuss these questions. Keep these questions on your phone and reflect while you are feeding your baby. Take ten minutes to journal while baby naps or a trusted person watches your baby. Talk to your baby about it. They'll love hearing your voice. Talk to your partner. Process with a therapist.

What are/were my expectations about my transition to motherhood?

What influenced these expectations?

What am I noticing now?

What is the hardest part for me?

How could I be gentler with myself?

What do I need?

What is the smallest, easiest step I could take to meet that need?

IDENTIFY YOUR PERSONAL STRENGTHS

Defining your strengths as a person can help you understand what makes you *you*, even if your world is changing. This can be a great way to get around the attachment to what you *do* as defining you and to connect more to who you *are*—a grounded stance when your capacity to do things as usual may become limited with a baby. You can reflect on your strengths on your own, ask your friends/partner/coworkers to share what your strengths are, or take a free ten-minute quiz to define your character strengths here: www.ViaCharacter.org. (You'll then receive a free report of your strengths or can purchase a more extensive one.) Examples of strengths include: curiosity, perseverance, honesty, humor, kindness, leadership, empathy, flexibility, logic, patience, resourcefulness, and perspective.

WAYS TO WORK IT IN

Discover strengths along with your partner, a friend, or another mom. Choose a small thing to do each day that makes you feel connected to one of your strengths. Find ways to use your strengths with your baby. Request twenty minutes for yourself to reflect on your strengths and make a plan for staying in touch with your most important ones. Share your plan for staying connected with strengths with someone to boost accountability.

What are my personal strengths?

Which of these strengths do I feel most authentically reflects who I am?

Which strengths do I most want to stay connected with?

What makes me feel like I am engaging my strengths?

How can my strengths serve me in motherhood?

What are small and accessible ways I can stay connected to my strengths with a new baby? (For example, if one of your strengths is humor, you can be silly with your baby, keep watch for amusing things happening throughout the day and note them in your phone or journal, or text a friend something that will make them laugh.)

TAKEAWAYS

1. Becoming a mother is a significant developmental transition, *matrescence*, touching many aspects of our lives.
2. The transition to becoming a mother may present new facets of your identity, and you can choose what congruence looks like for you and where to lean in. Identifying the most important parts of you can help you feel more grounded through the changes, when what you "do" in a day looks different and may become limited.

3. Tune in to the process of matrescence and what you need in response. Through giving yourself space and grace to experience it, you are liberated from feeling like there is something wrong about the grief, loss, and gravity matrescence may bring up.

Understanding the significance of matrescence can feel both daunting and empowering. It gives a name to the reality of becoming a mother and places your hands on the steering wheel. Becoming a mother is a process of becoming a new version of you.

The following chapters are dedicated to navigating matrescence and will continue to guide you. The next chapter explores the value of loosening our ties to what we "should" do as new mothers based on outside pressures from books, blogs, your mother-in-law, or that Instagram account you follow.

YOU SHOULD BE BY THE BOOK

———

"Stop. Reading. Books!" my husband pleaded with me. I was reading and reading and reading—about different parenting theories, sleep strategies, how to create an enriching baby environment… I wanted to find *the* best way to do things as a mom. If I could follow the books, maybe I could avoid my ultimate fear: screwing this up. Instead, I created such high expectations based on the advice I read, it became unrealistic to follow it all. The more rules I bought into, the more anxious I became. My husband started lovingly yanking books out of my hands.

It wasn't just books. There were suggestions from well-meaning mom friends, providers, and even strangers. I battled against my own preconceived notions of how I would approach aspects of parenting. For example, I received the loveliest assortment of cloth diapers as a gift from my dear friend and had every intention of using them exclusively. After having my first baby I was so overwhelmed with everything else, it became too much. I couldn't use those diapers.

But I wasn't able to just let the idea go and have compassion for myself in the process. I had to dig through layers of guilt about not doing this thing I committed to in my mind before even having a baby. *I'm not being earth conscious. My friend will be disappointed. I can't believe I'm so overwhelmed that I'm not able to manage using these diapers.*

The pressure of so many "shoulds" about parenting were closing in on me and creating a rigid approach in my parenting. Breast is best. Get the baby on a schedule. Start toilet training at four months. Get baby to sing. Teach baby a second language… People have distinct and vocal opinions on every aspect of raising a child. The downfall of rigid thinking is it does not serve us when our experiences fall out of line or the advice doesn't suit our needs. It's a distraction from the important work of motherhood.

Sometimes, research and reading are helpful and warranted. But it needs to be at the appropriate times and in the appropriate balance. And the best rule of all? Be flexible. The most important voice? Your own. Even if you don't know much about babies. Or feel like you're not doing it right. So long as your baby is safe and cared for, your intuition is the best voice to listen to.

THE REFRAME: THERE'S NO ONE RIGHT WAY

No matter what books, neighbors, or strangers in the grocery store tell you, there is no single correct way to do parenting. The way *you* decide is best and most manageable will be just fine. Holding yourself to a standard that feels strained or inauthentic based on advice or a book is unnecessary.

WHY WE SEEK OUTSIDE INFORMATION

Why are we listening to or looking for advice in the first place? One explanation: The current generation of moms knows how much parenting and early childhood matter.

A trend has grown since the 1990s toward "intensive parenting," an approach stressing the importance of early childhood experiences and getting informed by experts (Cain Miller 2018). Current parents want to build positive parent-child relationships, show love and unconditional support, and protect their children's physical and mental health, according to a recent Pew Research study (Hurst et al. 2023). In addition, "Today's parents feel intense pressure to constantly teach and interact with their children, whereas previous generations spent more time doing adult activities when their children were around" (Cain Miller 2023).

The difference between styles of parenting in previous generations and present day leaves some mothers without a template and with a knowledge gap to fill. About half of parents report they are raising their children differently than how they were raised (Hurst, Braga, et al. 2023). At the same time, other social pressures push in. Parents feel judged by their partners, parents, in-laws, friends, and other parents about how they raise their kids (Minkin and Horowitz 2023, 10). Lastly, we are seeking a predictable and reliable way to parent. In a review-based world, we want to find the five-star approach. The stakes are high in parenting, we want to do right by our kids, and we're looking for the best way to do it.

FILTERING YOUR SOURCES

If you find yourself scrolling through endless online search results, or unproductively paging through a stack of books like I did, you may need boundaries around your information-seeking. Here are some options to put this into action:

- **Pick and choose**: Some advice from books, family, and friends can be like nuggets of gold. Other times, it feels like lead weighing you down and holding you to a standard that's not a good fit. Choose the right nuggets for you and set the rest aside. Even if it's a bestselling book. Even if everyone in your mom's group swears by it.
- **Identify reputable sources**: Where can you get trusted information? Identify the people, professionals, books, and websites that feel helpful and affirm what you value *and* don't throw you into a spin. Maybe you need to avoid open-ended searches on the web.
- **Clarify the goal**: What are you really wishing to accomplish? Consider the best source to reach your goal and turn there first.
- **Back to basics**: Get focused on the core things you and your baby need, such as food, safety, closeness, physical comfort, sleep, and play. Meeting these needs is the intent, not meeting excessive standards.
- **Limit the intake**: If you tend to over-research or get locked into rigid thinking, seek answers specifically when you have a question or problem. When you look for information, take it in with curiosity, not as a directive.
- **Enlist help**: Ask a partner, friend, family member, or trusted professional to share the responsibility of researching and decision making so you don't get too bogged down,

paralyzed, or stuck in a research rabbit hole. You don't have to be in this alone.

LETTING GO

I asked moms, What is something you *thought* you should do as a new mom, but you ended up letting go because it didn't serve you? Here is a compilation of the survey responses:

Breastfeed
Pump breast milk
Bottle feed
Follow a schedule
Make baby food from scratch
Sleep separately
Co-sleep
Be active on social media
Baby play dates
Listen to/read all the advice
Work
Work full time
Not work
Take more time off with baby
Be perfect
Work out
Get professional baby photos
Take monthly photos of baby growing
Outings with friends
Join mom groups
Baby wearing
Keep up the appearance of having it all together
Have a baby shower

Keep a clean house
"Cry it out" sleep training
Be the mom my sisters were
Sleep when the baby sleeps
Travel, camping
Use cloth diapers
Baby potty training
Vaginal delivery
Constantly engage with/entertain my children
Clean eating
Keep up prior personal life
Say yes to things
Compare my child's milestones with others
Baby led weaning
Everything organic
Church
Get my pre-baby body back
Buy expensive stuff
Be creative and crafty
No screen time
Take the baby lots of places
Basically everything

This list has contradictions and things you may not agree with. What doesn't work for one mom will be exactly what helps another thrive. That's the point. We all have different needs, unique babies with their own temperaments, and distinct life circumstances. For this reason, we need to choose what works for us.

RECOGNIZING "SHOULDS"

Woven into many narratives I heard from clients were "shoulds"—how things need to be done a certain way because of internal or external expectations, pressures, or information. Maybe it's reading a book about getting baby on a schedule, or how a friend swears by a method for transition to solid foods. This input gets translated to a set of rules for how things "should" be done and are expected to play out—and emotional consequences if the rules are broken or the goals are not met.

One client shared she and her husband had opposite views on feeding their second baby. She struggled with breastfeeding her first child and it became highly stressful. During her second pregnancy, she wanted to bypass breastfeeding if it proved as hard as the first time. Her husband deeply wanted their second baby breastfed, and a big "should" hung between them. "How do I tell him I don't want to breastfeed?" she asked. It was a complex issue because the pressure of what she "should" do rubbed against what she really wanted for herself.

"Shoulds" block us from critical parenting assets: our needs, values, and intuition. They get their power from the strong emotions behind them, muddling our ability to make clear decisions. Here are the emotions I observe motivating shoulds, indicators of a disconnect from our authentic wisdom:

- **Guilt**: I am doing something bad or wrong if I don't fit the expectations, so I should…
- **Perfectionism**: If I get it wrong, I am defective and will be judged, so I should…

- **Shame**: If I fail, I am unworthy of connection, belonging, or love, so I should…
- **Comparison**: I want to measure up to or do better than those around me, so I should…
- **Approval-Seeking**: I long to fit in and be accepted, so I should…

These feelings suck the life out of decision making and turn choices into rigid rights and wrongs. Do you hear your own internal voice in any of these examples? There are antidotes to shoulds: allowing decisions to be dictated by your own values and intuition and building in flexibility.

PARENTING FROM VALUES

Your values are a resource for creating your own guidelines in motherhood. Think of values as your compass to find direction in making meaningful decisions for yourself and your family. Getting clear on values helps by:

- Distinguishing what you want from what you think you "should" do based on outside pressures;
- Choosing goals and feeling motivated to act toward them;
- Seeing past unpleasant emotions (like the ones above); and
- Assessing where change is necessary (Vyskocilova, Prasko et al. 2015, 46–48).

Let's say one of your parenting values is connection. You read a great book about sleep training telling you to put your baby down in their crib and let them cry. When you try it, your baby's cry is like nails on the chalkboard of your soul. But you think, *I should let her cry, because the book said thousands of babies have been taught to put themselves to sleep this way.* You're sitting outside your baby's door, and now *you're* starting to cry. This isn't working. You decide to step back and allow your values to guide you. Your value of connection comes to mind and is a reminder that more important than the words in a book is your connection with your baby. You open the door and pick your baby up from the crib and rock them to sleep. This feels more aligned with your values and the parent you want to be today. If you choose, you may try sleep training again another day—or not.

The point of the story is not to dissuade you against sleep training (which you may decide is exactly right for you), but to illustrate how you can use values as your North Star. See the exercises at the end of the chapter for an opportunity to define your values and start using them.

ATTUNING TO INTUITION

I asked Dawn Dickerson, a lactation consultant, parent educator, yoga instructor, and birth story listener, how she helps parents manage expectations and information intake. She said her work often involves "figuring out the actual goal and what is in the way. Many times, it is people's own rules that are in their way." Other times, "societal norms and expectations are against what parents feel they should do," and they think they're doing something wrong when it doesn't work. She will ask, "I wonder why you made that rule, and how it helped you in the past? I wonder where it came from. How is it a problem for you now?"

If we strip the "rules" away, what else can we hear? This is the space where our own intuition comes to the surface. By intuition, I mean inner wisdom, a deep sense of knowing, a feeling from your gut or heart. It is the voice that is separate from judgment and criticism and comes just from *you*. This voice can guide you when you are seeking answers and is always available to you when you want to tune into it. I'll show you how in the exercises at the end of the chapter.

THE POWER OF FLEXIBILITY

Flexibility is a motherhood superpower. If suggestions, plans, goals, or structures are not working, a new plan can be the best choice. Change gears. Get a new perspective. Try again later. Take the part that works for you and leave the rest. Scrap it altogether.

Two good questions to lean into flexibility are: What am I risking if I do things a different way? What am I risking if I keep doing the same thing? Often this will clarify if more is at risk by changing course or continuing in the same direction.

Take cues from yourself and your baby. Is this working for you both right now? Does this effort match your capacity today? If it's causing you significant stress that is hard to manage, or your baby seems to not get on board after several attempts, take a break and try again later. Set a goal if that feels helpful to let it go in the present, such as "This isn't working for me right now, but I'd like to try again in two to four weeks."

IDENTIFY YOUR PARENTING VALUES

Naming your parenting values creates a map to guide you through your decisions and keep you grounded in what matters to you. Look at the list of values below to get you started and add your own. You can choose as many as you like that feel important, authentic, and aligned with how you want to be as a parent. Return to your list when you need to be guided back to your intentions.

WAYS TO WORK IT IN

Work on your list in quiet moments. Break it up into multiple sessions if needed. Talk values through with a trusted friend, therapist, or spiritual director. Make a list together with your partner and see where you have common ground and a shared set of values. Consider any values you want to carry forward from your upbringing or parenting role models—even fictional ones from a book or movie.

List your parenting values here, using these examples to get you started:

Acceptance	Bravery
Accountability	Caring
Achievement	Challenge
Adventure	Cleanliness
Appreciation	Collaboration
Autonomy	Comfort
Awareness	Commitment
Balance	Compassion

Connection

Consistency

Contribution

Courage

Creativity

Credibility

Curiosity

Decisiveness

Dedication

Dependability

Determination

Discipline

Efficiency

Empathy

Encouragement

Energy

Enthusiasm

Equality

Ethics

Fairness

Faith

Family

Fearlessness

Flexibility

Forgiveness

Freedom

Fun

Generosity

Grace

Gratitude

Growth

Happiness

Harmony

Healing

Health

Honesty

Humility

Humor

Imagination

Inclusion

Independence

Individuality

Innovation

Inspiration

Intelligence

Intuition

Joy

Justice

Kindness

Leadership

Learning

Logic

Love

Loyalty

Maturity

Mindfulness

Modesty

Motivation

Open-mindedness

Optimism

Organization

Originality

Passion

Patience

Peace

Persistence

Playfulness

Preparedness

Proactiveness

Productivity

Purpose

Reflection

Relaxation

Reliability

Religion

Resilience

Resourcefulness

Responsiveness

Risk taking

Rules

Safety

Security

Self-awareness

Self-control

Service

Simplicity

Sincerity

Spirituality

Spontaneity

Stability

Strength

Structure

Sustainability

Synergy

Teamwork

Thoughtfulness

Timeliness

Tradition

Trust

Trustworthiness

Truth

Understanding

Uniqueness

Versatility

Vision

Vitality

Warmth

Wellbeing

Wisdom

CONNECT WITH YOUR INTUITION

Intuition is the deep knowing that comes only from you—not from external pressure or internal judgment. It's not a story, criticism, or fear. It is simply knowing.

Attuning to intuition is another way to cut through the noise around you and stay grounded in what you need and know is right. If you could use practice connecting with your intuition, try the questions below to get in touch with your unique intuition signals. Tuning in may require presence—calm and quiet so you can clearly hear your intuitive voice. Carve out a moment to sit quietly and take a few deep breaths. With practice, it becomes easier to notice intuition anytime.

WAYS TO WORK IT IN

Claim five quiet minutes for practice—during your baby's nap, before bed, on a bench during a walk, in a parked car, or while a trusted person watches your baby.

Think of a time you felt your intuition or inner knowing. Even if you're not sure, make your best guess. What did you notice when it happened?

How did your body signal that intuition was speaking? Maybe the hair stood up on your arms, you felt expansion in your chest, your scalp tingled, a thought floated to the surface, or you had a dream while sleeping. Were there other times when intuition felt different? List all the cues here. These are your personal intuition signals.

Practice intuition check-ins regularly. Take a quiet moment to clear your mind and check for any of your signals. What is your intuition telling you? If nothing is present, practice asking yourself what you need right now. Let the answer come to you.

Consistent practice helps strengthen your ability to listen to intuition, so it is readily available when you need it. Pair an intuition check-in with a cue to make it easier to remember to practice, such as bedtime, lunch, baby's second nap, etc., on a schedule that works for you.

TAKEAWAYS

1. Books, theories, and suggestions from friends and family are important resources, but no one method fits all.
2. Modern parenting is more demanding than in previous generations. Adding rigid rules, structures, and expectations out of alignment with your values turns up the pressure and adds stress.
3. Values-based choices, flexibility, and attuning to intuition are assets to motherhood and workarounds to getting stuck in rigid thinking or buried under books and advice.

There are almost as many alluring theories and ideas about baby rearing as there are baby products on the market. The sheer amount of information available can become crushing when research and advice go unchecked. Observe what boundaries you need and how it feels to cultivate your values, tend to your intuition, and experiment with flexibility. Write your motherhood story from your own perspective.

Keep reading to discover why motherhood coming "naturally" is a myth, and explore new ways to think about parental instinct.

MOTHERHOOD MYTH #3:
IT ALL COMES NATURALLY

I thought breastfeeding would come completely naturally. The baby and I would know what to do, and the feeding magic would happen. I read about latch, cabbage leaves, and mastitis. Sounded weird, but I was on board.

When I gave birth to my first baby, the nurses at the hospital almost immediately wanted me to start nursing. To my surprise, it was more complicated than I expected. Getting the latch right, wondering if the baby got any milk, finding a position that wasn't painful… They all felt like new and difficult tasks. I had a lactation consultation in the hospital but felt so concerned and lost about feeding I stayed in the hospital an additional night. At home, I tried finding my way with breastfeeding but still needed professional guidance.

It took several weeks to establish a routine that didn't cause excruciating pain and several months before breastfeeding felt like a "natural" experience. It wasn't because my innate wisdom finally surfaced. It was because I worked hard at it, learned through my experiences, and sought help. But because I had the expectation breastfeeding would come naturally to me, I felt so disappointed, confused, and ashamed when it seemed this natural ability was not bestowed on me.

For some women, it's not breastfeeding that is hard but bonding with their baby, or figuring out how to "play" with a being who gives little feedback in response in the early weeks. Maybe none of these things will be hard for you. But, just in case, I'd like to call the beginning of motherhood what it is instead of setting the expectation it will all be "natural": a huge learning curve. This way, you can avoid those shameful feelings you're somehow the only woman in the world without the capacity for immediate maternal instinct.

In her *New York Times* article, "Maternal Instinct Is a Myth That Men Created," Chelsea Conaboy describes motherly instinct as a concept that began with the Bible. The Industrial Revolution, capitalism, influential theorists such as Darwin, and politics contributed to how the concept looks now and remains ingrained in the definition of motherhood. This myth frames moms as the only ones who can have instinct about their children. It also "sustains outdated ideas about masculinity that teaches fathers that they are secondary—assistants, babysitters—and encourages mothers to see them that way, too" (Conaboy 2022).

Despite longstanding beliefs about maternal instinct, Conaboy points to new neuroscience to reveal something different: parents' brains adapt over time in response to exposure to their babies. Our brains are primed for change during parenthood, and this goes for all parents, regardless of gender. "The parental brain is changed, and it's also changeable—made more plastic than at most other points in adulthood. And while the biological mechanisms for change are quite different for gestational and non-gestational parents, scientists now believe that the outcomes may be similar for anyone—including fathers, adoptive parents and nonbinary parents—who truly invests time and attention in caregiving" (Conaboy 2022). How fascinating that our brains are growing and adapting with the experience of parenthood! And what a relief it's not just moms who have this capability. A natural process is at play here, but it's not just that women are programmed for baby care. It's learning.

THE REFRAME: IT COMES WITH LEARNING

If things aren't coming "naturally" in motherhood, you're not alone. Taking care of a baby and being a mother are entirely new skillsets that require building experience and knowledge over time. Mastery takes learning and practice, just like starting a new job or learning a new sport.

EVEN ANIMALS LEARN

Dawn Dickerson, lactation consultant and parent educator, shared with me that even animals need to learn how to breastfeed and care for their babies. "Breastfeeding and parenting are socially learned skills. So, if you don't have experience with that, you can't expect to know—because how would you?" she said.

In 2021, an orangutan at the Metro Richmond Zoo named Zoe had her first baby. Zoe had no exposure to other orangutans raising their young. When her baby was born, she refused to nurse or hold it close, and zookeepers stepped in to care for him. With her second baby in 2022, zookeepers showed Zoe videos of other orangutan mothers giving birth and taking care of their infants. A zookeeper gave Zoe a live breastfeeding demonstration with her own four-month-old child. Twenty-four hours after the demonstration, Zoe started breastfeeding her second baby (Hedgpeth 2023).

Other animal stories like Zoe's exist. If animals, which we can assume are more connected with "instincts" than humans, need help learning how to parent, perhaps we can have more compassion with ourselves when we need help learning too.

HEAR IT FROM MOMS

When I asked moms to share what didn't come as naturally as they expected in motherhood, several common themes emerged in survey responses:

- Breastfeeding (mentioned in 45 percent of responses)
- Getting baby to sleep
- Immediate love/connection/bonding/attachment with baby
- Baby care/competency as a parent
- Patience; tolerance for baby's crying
- Birth; healing from birth
- Coping with lack of sleep; sleeping when needed
- Postpartum weight loss
- Balancing work and motherhood
- Playing with baby
- Managing desire for time with and without baby
- Adjusting to motherhood

Additional comments tell us more:

"Learning to juggle life. It is a constant effort."
—ANONYMOUS, SAN FRANCISCO, CALIFORNIA

"Keeping a routine."
—ANONYMOUS, SAN DIEGO, CALIFORNIA

"Feeding the baby and teaching them how to sleep. Some babies don't sleep much. Our newborn took twenty-six-minute naps and only if being walked in the stroller."
—JENNA

"Parenting with my husband."
—ANONYMOUS, SAN DIEGO, CALIFORNIA

"Feeling like I was enough, doing a good job."
—ANONYMOUS, TEXAS

"Attuning to your kid. Knowing how to help your kid regulate things."
—ANONYMOUS, MASSACHUSETTS

"Bonding. I just thought you had a baby and felt over the moon excited. I came to realize after therapy and other growing moments, my parents neglected my basic needs, and I wasn't given tools to bond with my children. It took practice and patience."
—MADDIE

Some mothers noted things did come naturally for them. The experiences are as unique as we are.

PRIMING YOUR MINDSET

Psychologist Carol S. Dweck developed the concept of "growth mindset." She discovered some people have a "fixed mindset," believing abilities such as intelligence are fixed. Others have a "growth mindset," believing abilities can be developed with effort and learning.

Each group has a different view of success and failure. In the fixed mindset, success is "proving you're smart or talented" and failure is proof you're not, gauging your worth and competence. For growth mindset, success is about stretching to learn something new, and failure is "not growing. Not reaching for the things you value. It means you're not fulfilling your potential" (Dweck 2016, 15–16). Which group flourishes more? Which can readily ask for help when needed? Growth mindset.

From a fixed mindset perspective, mothers have static abilities, like natural instincts. If they don't manifest, it's failure and a reflection on us as mothers. A growth mindset offers space for learning and adapting to meet our motherhood potential. Challenges and setbacks aren't disasters. They are part of the process.

We have the ability to shift our mindset at any time. If you wish to lean into a growth perspective, try these tools:

- **Clarify your goals**: Find a specific focus, such as, "Today, I'll try for a solid breastfeeding latch," or "I will call a lactation consultant to get help in the morning."
- **Ask**: What did I learn? How can I grow? What do I need help or support with? Learning, effort, accessing help, and failed attempts are the path to mastery, not shortcomings.
- **Experiment**: A great way to loosen up rigid thinking and fixed mindset, experiments are playful, flexible, and leave room for modification. They have purpose: to help you learn and gather data, so you don't have to get caught up in you doing it wrong or failing. The exercises at the end of the chapter offer more on this.
- **Utilize resources**: Look at the list in the next section for options.

RESOURCES AVAILABLE TO HELP YOU

When you need help in your journey, use available resources. Asking for help is not a negative reflection on you. You don't have to do it all alone.

- Lactation consultation
- Lactation group
- Postpartum doula
- Parent educator
- Sleep consultant

- Nanny
- Mother's helper
- Babysitter
- Night nurse
- Support group
- New mother's group
- Pediatrician
- Parenting groups and classes
- Books
- Reputable blogs

KISS YOUR BRAIN

One of my son's teachers would say, "Kiss your brain! It's working hard," when my son got frustrated with an assignment. As new mothers, we could all use a kiss on the brain—a kind acknowledgment of how hard we are working and the growth it is producing. What kind messages can you give yourself about your hard work as a mother? How can you turn your attention toward the wins in your day?

EXERCISES FOR REFRAMING

RUN EXPERIMENTS

Framing tasks or behavior changes as "experiments" offers a perspective shift toward curiosity and flexibility. If I say, "What if you try an experiment this week?" versus "How are you going to change that behavior?" I get a very different reaction. When you encounter challenges in motherhood, see if an experiment can loosen the grip of expectations, rigid thinking, and resistance.

Try experiments when you feel resistant to change or gridlocked on what to do next. Enlist the help of a partner, friend, professional, or family member to support you in your experiments or tracking and making sense of your "results." Talk over experiment options with your partner or describe them to your baby.

DESIGNING AN EXPERIMENT:

1. Identify the change you are seeking. What would help you feel lighter, more proficient, or more at ease? What is the goal?
2. What action might help you move in the direction of your goal?
3. Define the smallest, easiest bite of this action you could try to inform if you want to continue or take a different action. This will be the experiment.
4. Decide when your experiment will start and how you will know it is producing the results you want. Define a checkpoint to assess your results and design a new experiment if needed.

ACKNOWLEDGE YOUR ACCOMPLISHMENTS

To access positive thinking about your mothering, acknowledge what you have accomplished daily. Accomplishments don't need to be big or perfect. How did you challenge yourself in a new way, or what were you able to do despite sleep deprivation or while juggling work and parenting? Some days it feels hard, so keep it simple: "I took care of myself and my baby today," or "I brushed my teeth." Other days it feels easier, or you may have a big win, such as "We drove an hour to visit my grandma and introduced her to the baby."

Try to find three accomplishments to acknowledge daily. Notice how it feels to acknowledge yourself.

WAYS TO WORK IT IN

Pair it with a daily activity such as taking a walk, feeding or rocking the baby, going to the bathroom, or when you lay down to sleep. Share your accomplishments with a partner, family member, or friend—in person or by text. Keep a journal to list accomplishments. Note if it gets easier to identify them over time.

TAKEAWAYS

1. Being a mother doesn't always come "naturally," but rather requires learning new skills and adjusting to new challenges. This learning is available to anyone of any gender—not just women.

2. Adopting a "growth mindset"—knowing you are capable of learning, and sticking to it when things are difficult—versus a "fixed mindset"—you have fixed capabilities and shouldn't have shortcomings—can help with your outlook and self-compassion through this phase of life.

3. Many resources are available to you if aspects of parenthood are getting you stuck. You don't have to do it alone. It's reasonable to need help in this new endeavor.

You should not know how to be a parent instantaneously or "have it in you" naturally if you've never done it before. When we orient our expectation to learning instead, we can better match the actual experience of parenthood. Learning will take time, effort, and resources, but you are capable. Growth is success.

The next chapter explores the process of creating a "village" of support for your family. Keep reading if you're curious why you need a village and how it's built.

MOTHERHOOD MYTH #4:

THE VILLAGE SHOWS UP

———

"Where's my damn village?" I wondered a few weeks into motherhood.

Confession: Before birth, I wasn't convinced I needed a village. It sounded crowded and invasive, and I would be just fine on my own, thank you. In fact, I felt annoyed by the question, "Do you have help after the baby?" It was hard to conceptualize why I wouldn't be able to take care of a single baby on my own when I was lucky enough to have an abundance of resources like a home, a partner, stable income, and a marital and family therapy background—not to mention the baby classes, baby books, and gear. Why did people keep asking? Did it seem like I couldn't handle it?

A deeper confession: I also had difficulty trusting people. In my youth, I experienced parental abandonment and developed a belief that I wasn't worth showing up for. I honed my skills of independence. I often guarded my heart in relationships. Asking for help directly felt painfully vulnerable, like an intentional setup for rejection. By the time I reached motherhood, I had healed this wound, but the urge to avoid asking for help and fierce independence was still strong. So, when it came to creating a village, I thought, *Nope.* I would do this on my own just like everything else. I certainly wasn't going to ask people for help and risk the pain of them not showing up.

The support of a "village" wasn't necessary because of some inadequacy in my ability to care for a baby. It's necessary because taking care of a baby on your own is extremely exhausting and hard. The actual tasks of baby care can be mastered, but the constancy of doing those tasks around the clock, the sleep deprivation, the inability to do anything without your baby, the isolation, and the instantaneous disconnection from how you typically live your life are challenges difficult to resolve alone.

The only resource I arranged after my first baby was my husband, who took two weeks of leave from work and then was home part time for two weeks. We had visitors but not under the pretense of being helpful. When my husband went back to work, I felt so tired, isolated, and cut off from the life I knew. I resented him for being able to go to work and have so much freedom to move about his life, down to things like going to the bathroom whenever he pleased and not having a baby's cry interrupt his thoughts.

It began to dawn on me why "it takes a village to raise a child," but I hadn't created one. When I heard that phrase, it felt like a promise: It takes a village, so your village shows up. I hoped a system of support would spontaneously appear if I needed it. But I already sent out the message I would be fine on my own, and no assistance came knocking at my door. I felt foolish when I realized how badly I wished for help. I had a way out: to take charge and call in the village. When I did, things got a lot better.

THE REFRAME: CALL IN YOUR VILLAGE; YOU'LL BE GLAD YOU DID

Creating a supportive village is a way to ensure you have the resources you need to manage the demands of baby care and matrescence. A great village is one you thoughtfully create and call in. Ask so it shows up.

WHAT DOES "VILLAGE" MEAN?

"It takes a village to raise a child" is thought to be derived from a proverb present in several African cultures. The meanings include how it is a social responsibility to raise and teach children and how a *community* holds the space for children to grow up and thrive (Goldberg 2016).

While the traditional use of the term is child-focused, the village needs to support the family as a whole. I will offer up a definition of village for our purposes, and of course I'm going to put moms right at the center.

Village: The network of people supporting you (and your partner, if you have one) in raising your child. This may look different as needed over the course of parenthood and can include extended family, friends, caregivers, professionals, and the broader community.

WHY CONSIDER A VILLAGE

While "it takes a village" is a popular phrase, the societal undercurrent is still an expectation mothers can do everything on their own. This is reflected in medical and social policies, such as sending women home from the hospital in as little as twenty-four hours after delivery, with no further contact for up to six weeks.

Many parts of Asia and Europe have cultural and professional practices for supporting new mothers, such as a "confinement" period to allow a mother to rest and heal or home visits from health care professionals. "In contrast, the American culture is one of rugged individualism wherein postpartum mothers are often left without support from professionals or their families and friends… there is no professional support standard of care for women in America" (Corrigan, Kwasky, and Groh 2015, 49–50).

One mom contrasted delivering her first baby in the US and her second while living abroad:

"In Germany, I had a midwife come to my house every two days for two weeks, and then every week for the month after that. It was amazing to have someone during that isolating time just for me and to check in on my baby and either help or reassure that she was fine. I would have loved this for my first baby."

—ANONYMOUS, CALIFORNIA

Other women share their postpartum experiences:

"I remember feeling so unbelievably alone and isolated."

—BETSY C.

"I think I truly wasn't prepared for how much my body would need to recover while learning to care for the new little being and the pain of breastfeeding. My first spent eleven days in the NICU which was emotional and traumatic for both of us and then they just sent us home, alone, saying good luck."

—ANONYMOUS, CALIFORNIA

"We were pretty much at home all the time, very isolated from the world."

—ANONYMOUS, CALIFORNIA

A village can help reduce isolation, provide emotional support, give information about baby care, share the burden of household tasks, and offer parents needed breaks. Villages can also protect mental health. Increased levels of support have been shown to lower postpartum depression scores, and *lack* of support is a top risk factor for postpartum depression (Corrigan, Kwasky, and Groh 2015, 50).

A TYPICAL DAY IN MOTHERHOOD

It's hard to understand how life will look with a baby. Before kids, most of us are used to a life centered around ourselves and our own needs, primarily on a clock during our waking time. At the beginning of your child's life, you will be 100 percent responsible for meeting all their needs in addition to your own, on a twenty-four-hour clock. Even if you are educated about what a baby needs on paper, it's easy to underestimate the amount of time it will take. When they need to eat, you have to feed and burp them, when they poop you have to change them, when they need rest you soothe them to sleep, and if they are sick, you have to triage the condition and take them to the doctor.

I give an example below to illustrate a day in the life of mother. This is not a "schedule," and your baby will work on their own clock, based on their own unique needs, as guided by your pediatrician.

- **Diapering:** eight to twelve times per day at five to ten minutes each equals forty to 120 minutes per day
- **Feeding:** eight to twelve times per day at twenty to sixty minutes each equals 160 minutes to twelve hours per day
- **Burping:** eight to twelve times per day after feeding at five minutes each equals forty to sixty minutes per day
- **Soothing to sleep:** nine to twelve times per day (ten to thirty minutes each) equals ninety minutes to six hours per day
- **Play:** during baby's wakeful periods, a few minutes each time equals twenty to sixty minutes per day
- **Cleaning up additional bottles/pump items/clothing/ diapers generated by baby:** twenty-plus minutes per day
- **Incidentals:**
  - Soothing your baby when they are upset or fussy for no reason
  - Cleaning up a diaper blowout or spit up
  - Bathing baby: fifteen to thirty minutes, three times a week

- ○ Cluster feeding: add extra feedings to the count above
- ○ Missed nap: subtract from your free time
- ○ Researching a new health concern, solution, or developmental phase
- ○ Baby well check or doctor's visit for health concern

The time adds up! This totals six hours on an easy day and a maximum of almost a whole day. If we average the two, the total is fourteen hours of baby care per day.

Baby care will fill a significant amount of your waking time and continue during times you are not typically awake. An additional shift is how time will be segmented between meeting the baby's needs. Before the baby, you could do one task continuously and when you chose. After the baby, your available time is sandwiched in smaller windows between meeting your baby's needs.

As you grow into motherhood, it becomes easier to integrate baby care tasks into the flow of the day and accomplish other things in tandem with caring for a baby. But it is still demanding. Support for breaks and assistance with baby care and household tasks from your village can ease the transition to parenthood significantly.

THE ANATOMY OF A VILLAGE

Who is in a village? That's totally up to you. Some people will be invited, some will wander in, and others will need to be kept out. Here are some examples of roles to consider when calling in your village:

Advisors:

A trusted pediatrician
Experienced moms who can offer sage advice
Baby care/parent educator
Lactation consultant
Sleep coach

Healers:

OBGYN/midwife
Physical therapist specializing in women's issues, pelvic
floor
Psychiatrist
Acupuncturist
Reiki practitioner
Massage therapist

Helpers:

Family, friends, neighbors who can give you breaks by watching the baby to allow you to rest or do something for you

Family, friends, neighbors who can help with tasks such
as picking up groceries, bringing meals, running errands,
cleaning

Fellow moms with whom you can take turns watching each
other's babies

Housekeeper
Meal delivery service

Grocery delivery/pickup service
Mother's helper
Nanny
Babysitter
Postpartum doula
Night nurse

<u>Supporters:</u>

Friends, family, neighbors who will listen
Moms to gather with and share experiences
A new mom's group
A MOPs (mothers of preschoolers, infants, or toddlers)
group
Therapist
Birth story listener
Support group/therapy group

RESISTANCE TO VILLAGE-BUILDING

If you're still not convinced a village is for you, you're not alone. Many factors contribute to resistance to asking for support. Some mothers reported not wanting to burden others, their needs were not understood, asking felt like extra work when they were already tired, or a social network was not available. Many mothers received cultural or family messages emphasizing independence or having it all together.

"I didn't have a person I could trust."

—ANONYMOUS, SAN DIEGO, CALIFORNIA

"It is not easy to ask for help. Especially with being Latina and feeling pressured to do it all yourself, there is a lot of pressure to keep up appearances."

—GRACE A.

"I felt embarrassed and didn't want anyone to know I was struggling or didn't know what to do. I felt that it was my 'job' since I wasn't working, so to ask for help meant that I can't do my job. Failure."

—ANONYMOUS, CALIFORNIA

"I was raised by parents who never asked for help. Their biggest desire was for me to be strong, and at the time, I thought it was stronger to do things on my own."

—BRIDGET K.

"I wasn't surrounded by family or those who understood/ supported my motherhood goals."

—ANONYMOUS, SAN FRANCISCO, CALIFORNIA

A key part of village-building is making it work for you. Here are some pointers:

- **Make it on your terms**: Only invite support that truly feels helpful and positive.
- **Get creative with where you look**: Would coworkers, neighbors, or members of your faith community be a good fit? If you're a military family, what supportive ser-

vices for new families are available? Would online support feel more within reach? Is it possible to pay for services such as a postpartum doula or a cleaning service? Expand beyond just your family if that's not a good resource.

- **Build it in**: Dawn Dickerson, lactation consultant and parent educator, advocates for "helpful visits" when baby arrives. This creates clear parameters that anyone coming to see the baby will also be expected to pitch in and provide a little help.
- **Be clear about what you need**: Ask directly for what you are looking for. Put it in writing if that helps, such as posting a list of tasks like sweeping or folding laundry.
- **Be flexible**: If you try once and it doesn't work out, don't give up. Maybe there is another person or task you can ask for next time. Things may not be perfect when done by someone else, but see if you can allow "done" to be good enough.
- **Ask now, decide later**: If you're not sure what kind of help you will need, you can ask for help to be "on call" so you can engage support when you need it.

Motherhood is a marathon, and building the skill of asking for help early will smooth the path for later, when you need a sitter or help with school pickup. Continue with the following exercises for more ways to bust through resistance.

EXERCISES FOR REFRAMING

VISUALIZE YOUR VILLAGE

Here is an opportunity to imagine the type of village you could build. If you are feeling resistant, just experiment with the questions and see if anything useful comes up.

If you are in a partnered relationship, try this exercise together to include their emotional, social, and practical needs as well. This way, you can both be supported and more likely be available to each other and to your baby.

WAYS TO WORK IT IN

Do a "ride along" with a current mom to get a sense of what parenthood looks like in real life so you can assess your needs. Brainstorm with a friend or family member the type of help you might like and who is a fit. Discuss with your partner over lunch, dinner, or a baby's nap.

Becoming a parent creates new demands, presents constraints on your time, and requires physical healing if you are birthing. What are, or do you anticipate will be, the hardest parts for you?

What support would bring more ease to these areas?

What other support would you like to receive? How does calling in support align with your values from chapter two?

What beliefs might you need to release to allow yourself to accept support? For example: ideas passed on from my family that do not serve me; I must have control over how things are done.

Who can meet your needs for support?

What help do you need to access support? For example: collecting funds for hiring a postpartum doula, or have my partner send some messages out to ask for support.

INVITE YOUR VILLAGE

Okay, here's where you take the step of asking and inviting. If this feels vulnerable, take a baby step, such as signing up for meal delivery service or texting your friend who you know will say yes. See if you can build some trust and momentum from there to fill out your village, however big or small you would like it. Think of "no" as "next." Find the next option that may work for you if one doesn't pan out.

Try inviting one person a day to start. Challenge another mom to call in support for herself along with you and encourage each other's village-building. Ask friends or family for their hidden helping talents to see who might match your needs.

Who would you like to invite to your village? How will you do it, and when?

Do you have to set boundaries, such as telling certain people you are not widely accepting visitors yet, requesting "helpful visitors" only, limiting the duration of visits, or placing a cooler outside to receive meals so you and baby are not disturbed?

Is there someone you would like as a "gatekeeper" or "coordinator" to manage a meal train, fend off unhelpful visits, or give updates on your behalf?

TAKEAWAYS

1. "It takes a village" is a commonly used phrase about child rearing that makes it sound like a village awaits us all once we have a child.
2. American mothers typically face a lack of support, and the village often needs to be built from the ground up.

3. Intentionally calling in a village is a way to reduce isolation, decrease depression, and help new parents cope with the demands of baby care.

Calling in support is a gift to you and your family to reduce stress, strain, and create more ease. Your village may be a person or two, or a whole posse, whatever feels right to you. You can always change, expand, or prune your village as your needs evolve or become clearer. Many new mothers feel isolated, but you don't have to do it alone. You deserve support. Help is available if you ask for it, even if it takes more than one ask.

Read on to find out about physical recovery from pregnancy and birth. We'll explore alternatives to the expectation for bodies to "bounce back." Take a stretch, grab a snack. You're doing great, mama.

MOTHERHOOD MYTH #5:
YOUR BODY BOUNCES RIGHT BACK

———

I told her I wasn't pregnant, but she blessed my "baby" anyway.

Carving out some needed time for relaxation, I scheduled a massage with a mobile massage therapist. She came in, set up her table in a bedroom, and asked me some initial questions. Was I pregnant? No. Any areas to focus on? Always my neck and shoulders. As the massage got started, we chatted a bit and she mentioned seeing my kids on her way in. I told her they were four and seven.

We quieted down and the massage was lovely, until the very end.

"I hope this has been healing and you have a great rest of your day. I want to bless you and your unborn baby—I think it's a boy. Be sure to drink lots of water today," she told me in a soft, soothing, your-massage-has-ended voice.

I found this both hilarious and mortifying. I wasn't pregnant. I already told her that. I handed her payment over and escorted her out the door as fast as possible. It seemed the way my body looked did not conform to her concept of how it should after having children, so she created her own story to explain my abdomen.

This wasn't the first time. Right after I had my son, someone asked when my baby was due. I told them: four weeks ago. A friend once asked when I was going to tell her "the news," looking expectantly at my belly. It is ingrained in our culture that bodies should look a certain way, and bodies bounce back to pre-baby form right after giving birth. But pregnancy and birth are significant physiological events.

Bouncing right back is an unrealistic expectation because recovery takes time, despite the images presented by social and traditional media. Celebrities are often praised for bouncing back when they have resources and professionals to make this happen. Recovery for each woman is unique based on her pregnancy, delivery, and body. But all of us are made of flesh and bone, not elastic.

THE REFRAME: YOUR BODY NEEDS TO HEAL

It took time and resources for your body to create a baby, and it will need time to heal and reconstruct from the demands of pregnancy and birth. Developing a mindset of taking care of and healing your body creates less distress than expecting it to "bounce back." While most body changes are temporary, others may be permanent, and some changes could need specific care.

TYPICAL BODY CHANGES AFTER HAVING A BABY

I've collected a list below of some common body experiences after delivering a baby. The purpose of this information is to help you build an understanding of physical recovery from pregnancy and birth, so you get a sense of what you need. Keep in mind I'm not a medical doctor, and this is not an exhaustive list. Your medical provider is the best source of information about your physical recovery. Contact them right away if you have concerns about your health or body after delivery. Many medical and birthing centers have a dedicated phone line to reach someone immediately if you have a medical concern postpartum.

For birthing mothers, body experiences immediately after delivery include:

- Vaginal bleeding, called lochia, for approximately four to six weeks (for both vaginal and C-section deliveries)
- Cramping
- Pain in back, neck, or joints
- Perineal pain
- Pain at C-section incision site
- Swollen breasts
- Bladder problems
- Bowel problems
- Hemorrhoids (ACOG 2020)
- Constipation
- Pain during urination and bowel movements
- Stretch marks
- "Mommy brain," a type of brain fog thought to be due to hormones, sleep disruption, or both
- Core weakness

- Breast and nipple pain/tenderness
- Changing body shape as body remodels from pregnancy and birth
- Exhaustion
- "Baby blues": feeling drained, ups and downs in mood, weepiness, sadness that is mild and resolves by two weeks postpartum (see chapter eight for more information about mood changes and postpartum mental health)

Common body experiences in later weeks and months include:

- Lack of menstruation for as long as twenty-four months (please note ovulation, and therefore pregnancy, can happen before your period resumes, so plan for birth control accordingly if you do not want another pregnancy at this time)
- Hair loss around three to six months due to hormone changes
- Decrease in sex drive and vaginal lubrication
- Sleep disruption/deprivation

Other changes experienced by *some* women include:

- Enlarged feet: due to relaxed muscles and ligaments
- Diastasis recti: separation of the abdominal wall
- Varicose veins
- Change in breast shape/fullness
- Pelvic floor weakness or prolapse
- Pain caused from new strains of baby carrying/wearing/feeding
- Pain caused by aggravation of previous conditions
- Difficulty losing all weight gained during pregnancy
- Lasting changes in body shape

- Thyroid problems
- Tendonitis

MOTHERS SHARE THEIR BODY EXPERIENCES

"My boobs are now pancakes."

—ANONYMOUS, SAN DIEGO, CALIFORNIA

"I weighed less after birth than I did when I got pregnant, but my pants didn't fit. My hips had shifted. So the idea that you can get your pre pregnancy body back was 100 percent impossible for me."

—ANONYMOUS, ARIZONA

"I became a woman and not a young girl."

—MADDIE

"Joint laxity and autoimmune flares—and the momma pouch in my belly area."

—AMANDA H.

"A shape that jeans don't seem to fit. Saggy breasts. Tired eyes."

—ALYSSA S.

"Peeing myself when I sneeze."

—JOANNA

"Easier to gain weight, harder to lose weight."

—ANONYMOUS, ARIZONA

"C-section scar."

—ANONYMOUS, SAN DIEGO, CALIFORNIA

"I did lose the baby weight, but it was at least nine months to get back to almost normal. I didn't lose the last ten pounds until I stopped breastfeeding."

—ANONYMOUS

"It was hard to ignore other mothers who proudly 'bounced back' and fit into their pre-pregnancy jeans. Two children later, I let go of the size/number I used to be and accepted that my body has evolved. I still struggle with accepting my body and try to practice compassion toward myself."

—JOY F.

EXPECTATIONS OF PHYSICAL RECOVERY

I interviewed Dr. Sheri DeSchaaf, DPT, about postpartum bodies. She's a mom and doctor of physical therapy specializing in women and pelvic floor treatment. I asked her what is reasonable to expect of women's postpartum physical recovery. She said, "The first piece of advice I give people is if the internet is stressing you out, stop looking at it. We never know if what we're seeing or reading or watching on social media is the whole story. Many people put all the good stuff out there because they want you to follow their page or buy their program… You don't know what they're not telling you."

Dr. DeSchaaf contrasts our expectations around postpartum recovery to other types of physical stress. "The expectation that we would feel normal after six weeks does not coincide with what we know or how we view any other musculoskeletal injury in the body," she said, referring to the typical clearance for physical activity at a six-week postpartum checkup. "If you have a really bad ankle sprain, your doctor will tell you it's probably going to take eleven to twelve weeks to heal. When you're pregnant, your body is under repetitive stress and strain for six to nine months, then at the end of it, you have an extremely strenuous event where you are pushing a large object through a very small muscular space." She added, "Eighty percent of first-time vaginal births are going to have some degree of tearing. For that soft tissue damage alone, we would expect a six- to twelve-week healing time."

All of this strain is more likely to take eleven to twelve weeks to heal for a vaginal delivery, according to Dr. DeSchaaf. For a C-section, she stressed this is a *major abdominal surgery.* For other types of surgery, "You're going to automatically get twelve to sixteen weeks of physical therapy, two to three times a week. No questions asked… With a C-section: Here's a cold pack to put in your underwear, and have fun taking care of your newborn." At six weeks postpartum, "most people don't feel normal. And then they feel ashamed that they don't feel normal because they feel like they did something wrong."

She suggests the initial weeks after delivery "should be a time of active rest and restoration, not you feeling like you should be doing what you were doing before pregnancy. Be very cautious with doing too much." If you are unsure, consulting with a physical therapist can answer questions, like, What can I do? What should I do? And how much? "It might not be the same as for your friend down the street or the account that you follow on Pinterest."

What red flags in physical healing indicate physical therapy is needed? Dr. DeSchaaf named the following:

- Any leakage from the bladder or bowel
- Feelings of vaginal or rectal bulging, pressure, or falling out, especially after three to four weeks postpartum.
- Pain with sexual intercourse after the fourth try. Pain should be gradually decreasing with every attempt at intercourse.
- Severe abdominal weakness or separation of the abdominal wall in the middle of your stomach after six weeks postpartum
- Pain of any kind related to body changes during pregnancy
- Fear, such as "I'm afraid to exercise, I'm afraid to lift my baby, I'm afraid to have sex." Physical therapy "can help people get back to their lives without fear by being educated, knowing more about their bodies, and helping address anything that is not right."

Treating problems early is best, as the longer you wait, "the more you have compensatory muscular and neuromuscular patterns, because your body's going to adapt." But if time has passed, it's not necessarily too late.

"I have lots of patients who call me and say, 'Oh, it's been three years since I had my baby' or 'ten years since I had my baby. Can this even still be fixed?' Well, it's certainly worth trying," said Dr. DeSchaaf.

Some patients require a mind-body approach to healing, such as women who experience an unplanned C-section or traumatic birth.

"There's usually quite a bit of psychoemotional trauma wrapped up in that. Mentally, the client might feel like they've dealt with it. But physically, their body is still hanging on to the fear and the trauma they experienced during the labor, and their muscles are guarding. So we need to help them process that and let it go."

Dr. DeSchaaf will refer patients to a mental health therapist alongside physical therapy if emotional and physical healing need to happen together to address the concerns. "You're a whole body, a whole person," and you may need to heal accordingly.

Because of the extent of physical recovery, "physical therapy is not standard postpartum, but it really should be." Trust yourself in your healing process, she says. Women know when something's not right.

If you seek treatment, she recommends finding a provider trained in perinatal concerns (and pelvic floor issues, if relevant). In many cases, physical therapy can be accessed directly, without the need for a physician's referral. Coming back to normal physical functioning can be a key part of feeling at home in matrescence, even if it's just getting back to a fitness routine.

"For a lot of women, returning to exercise is an enormous part of their stress relief and how they manage their mental health. When they can't exercise it just compounds their sense of despair and having lost themselves."

The primary message I heard from Dr. DeSchaaf is to expect recovery to be gradual. There is also hope and empowerment in her words: When something is not right, we can seek help, and healing is possible.

SUPPORTING POSTPARTUM HEALING

Postpartum recovery is not easy. But it is temporary, and we can do many things to be more comfortable and supported. It starts in our minds, with our perspectives and expectations.

Just as your body underwent a transformation to build a baby, it will again transform as it unwinds and heals from pregnancy and birth. Like the physical changes of adolescence—hormones, budding breasts, acne, moodiness, body hair and odors, menstruation—matrescence brings its own set of physical changes. With adolescence, body changes are largely accepted as an inherent part of moving from being a child to an adult. We can't hurry it up or skip over it.

What if we invite this perspective into matrescence? We could think of postpartum healing as a fundamental part of becoming a mother, when a body moves through pregnancy to a non-pregnant state. It happens over time. We can't fast-forward through it. Sometimes it's frustrating and embarrassing. But it is a necessary process for our bodies. This might bring more patience and understanding to replace the expectation of bouncing back in shape, weight, and functioning. We might even be able to appreciate the amazing work our bodies are doing. See the exercises at the end of the chapter for more on body appreciation.

Other ways to support postpartum healing include:

- **Rest**: Expect the most acute recovery in the initial weeks, a prime time for rest and minimizing your to-do list. How can you do less by delegating, outsourcing, or pausing tasks? Visit chapter four for more on calling in support and the types of help available.
- **Comfort measures**: Ice, warmth, a belly wrap, a shoulder rub from a willing partner or family member, talking to someone supportive, and positive distractions such as watching your favorite show can all increase your comfort. Experiment with what feels best to you.
- **Nutritious food**: A nourished body has a better foundation to heal. Cooking and freezing nutritious meals in advance, arranging a meal train for others to bring dinners, or setting up a meal delivery service are ways to support eating well. A nutritionist is a resource if you are struggling to identify the foods your body needs.
- **Limiting visitors**: Entertaining guests is not something you need to add to your plate until you are ready. Allow only visitors who are helpful or soul-quenching in your first postpartum weeks, or keep visits very brief so you can get back to rest.

- **Gentle movement**: Gradually bring in movement that feels good to your body, not punishing. When you are ready and as directed by your doctor, consider walking, yoga, or brief workout videos (many postpartum routines are available through fitness streaming services or YouTube). Start slow and easy, and follow your body's cues. Some gyms such as the YMCA offer childcare, and local exercise groups for moms can be found through Meetup.com.
- **Patience with weight loss**: Postpartum weight loss is typically a gradual process, and healing may initially be your body's most important task. If you are concerned about your weight, consult your doctor. Use caution with setting expectations based on social media or celebrities.
- **Additional support available:**
  - *OBGYN, midwife, or physician*: for any general concerns about the progress of your healing. Your care doesn't have to stop at your six-week checkup.
  - *Physical therapy*: to address specific functioning concerns, pain, or return to fitness routines (see the Expectations of Physical Recovery section above); seek a provider specializing in postpartum treatment.
  - *Lactation consultant*: for help with lactation concerns including painful breastfeeding and if you would like to stop breastfeeding or milk production.
  - *Postpartum doula*: for in-home support with baby care, healing, education, and help with light housework during your healing process.
  - *Dietitian/nutritionist*: for developing a healthy postpartum diet, understanding foods that support lactation, or developing a plan for weight management sensitive to postpartum healing. Seek a provider specializing in postpartum nutrition.

- *Acupuncture*: to support hormone balance, mood, and healing.
- *Postpartum massage*: may help with pain, swelling, relaxation, and healing; seek a provider specializing in postpartum massage.
- *Placenta encapsulation*: Research has not yet validated the benefit of placenta encapsulation, but possible benefits are improved mood, energy, milk production, and reduced bleeding (Johnson 2018, 846–852). Placenta must be properly handled and prepared by a reputable provider.

SPOTLIGHT ON SEX

When to resume sex after having a baby is entirely up to you. Many women receive a green light for intercourse by their provider at their six-week postpartum checkup, but that doesn't mean they're ready to go home and get busy. Postpartum intercourse may initially be painful due to healing from birth as well as hormonal changes causing vaginal dryness and low libido. Another factor draining sex drive is feeling "touched out" by baby care, leaving no more tolerance for physical touch. Fatigue, overwhelm, shifts in available time together, and difficulty reaching a relaxed state to cultivate sexual interest are other barriers. If intercourse is difficult, you don't have to suffer through just to please your partner. But navigating this effectively may require communication and creativity.

I tell my clients the postpartum phase is a great time to open communication about sex, because it's a new landscape with opportunities to develop new habits. Communication tends to enhance sex lives, not diminish them. Consider communicating about the following:

A constructive way to turn down sex: Affirm your interest in connection with your partner and define a point of re-connection, such as, "I'd like to be intimate with you, but I'm not ready yet. I'll check in with you (next week, after I start physical therapy, when I'm more rested, etc.)."

What you *are* interested in: If not intercourse, what physical intimacy sounds appealing? Holding hands, kissing, massage, cuddling, hugging, caressing? Not all sex has to be intercourse. As you are ready, try non-intercourse intimacy if you'd prefer.

How it's going in the moment: When you try intercourse, you may need to take it slow, so let your partner know how it's going and what you need.

When you're in the mood: Creating a signal to let each other know when you're interested in intimacy is a great way to increase your chances of using an available window to connect. This could be a code word, special wink, or just said.

How it can happen: If you used to have luxurious and lengthy sex or only had sex at night before the baby, maybe you can experiment with new ways that fit into your current lifestyle. In the morning? Lunchtime? Quick and to the point?

Remember, if intercourse is painful after several tries, reach out to your doctor or a physical therapist to evaluate your healing.

I'll reiterate that for most women, especially when breastfeeding, menstruation does not resume until weeks to months after delivery, or breastfeeding is stopped. Periods may also initially be irregular. Because it cannot be predicted when ovulation (and the ability to get pregnant) will happen before your period resumes regularly, it will be important to use birth control methods if you would like to prevent another pregnancy. My midwife shared one of her patients became pregnant again at only four weeks postpartum.

EXERCISES FOR REFRAMING

SET UP YOUR SUPPORT

Perhaps this chapter brought up new ideas or shifted your perspective on your postpartum healing process. Take a moment to evaluate your needs here and how you can get them met.

WAYS TO WORK IT IN

Discuss your recovery with your partner, a family member, or support person, and brainstorm together the best strategies for supporting your healing. Ask a trusted veteran mom about her healing process and what support might be useful for you. Think big—as if no limits exist to the amount of support you can receive—to open your mind to your options.

What needs do you anticipate around your postpartum healing process?

How could your needs be supported?

How can you get this support?

GIVE YOUR BODY APPRECIATION

Turning your mind toward appreciation has benefits for your mood and mindset. If frustration about your body is getting you down, try appreciating what *is* working for you about your body. Some examples:

My body created a baby.
My heart is beating, and my lungs are breathing all on their own.
My body is producing life-sustaining nourishment for my baby.
My body delivered a baby.
My brain is learning how to care for my child.

WAYS TO WORK IT IN

Ask your partner to chime in about the amazing things your body is doing. Write or post your appreciations in a visible place in your home as a touch point. Come up with body appreciations with another mom. Build accountability by exchanging texts of one body appreciation each day for a week with a friend or family member.

What words of appreciation could you offer yourself about your postpartum body?

TAKEAWAYS

1. Rather than an immediate "bouncing back," postpartum recovery is a gradual process of healing.
2. Healing is most acute in the initial weeks, and you may want extra support and boundaries at this time to allow you to rest. Being gentle with yourself, appreciating the work your body is doing, and setting reasonable expectations can counter the pressure to "bounce back."
3. Many supports and professionals are available to assist your healing. If something is not right in your recovery, reach out for help.

How your body heals after pregnancy and delivery will be unique to you and to each pregnancy you have, if more than one. It may feel frustrating or alarming to know the reality of postpartum recovery. The idea is to inform you so you know what to expect, empower you to access the support matching your needs, and encourage you to be gentle with yourself if "bouncing back" isn't happening how you thought it would. Despite being mistaken as pregnant years after having my last baby, I thank my body for doing the work of creating my two incredible kids.

In the next chapter I give special attention to new mothers' sleep—a topic seldom talked about in meaningful terms. You'll get a clear picture of what sleep changes to expect and tips for managing sleep disruption.

MOTHERHOOD MYTH #6:
SLEEP WHEN THE BABY SLEEPS

In my pre-motherhood mind, the sleep disruption caused by a new baby would be like staying up late to study or pulling an all-nighter with friends. The practical realities of a baby "waking in the night" and "feeding around the clock" made sense on paper, but I couldn't truly grasp what this was like until it happened.

It started about three days after my son was born. His crying would wake me in the middle of the night. My husband changed him, I fed and burped him, and then I rocked or walked him back to sleep. I would then try to get myself back to sleep. But the stimulation of being awake with lights on tricked my body into thinking it was daytime. Every little movement or utterance from the baby in the bassinet next to me disrupted my descent to sleep. Minutes, sometimes hours, would tick by before I fell asleep. By then, it was nearly time to wake up with the baby again. The process repeated two or three times per night.

After a week or two of this, I started doing funny things: putting the dish soap away in the refrigerator instead of the cupboard, accidentally shampooing my face instead of my hair in the shower, walking into a room and forgetting why

I was there. My husband and I called ourselves "SDPs," short for sleep-deprived parents, to label why we could no longer recall the name of someone we knew or how exasperating it was to identify what we wanted for dinner.

This long-term and repeated lack of sleep wasn't at all like staying up late to party. I was *deeply* and *desperately* tired. I didn't have space in my life to catch up because the cycle happened again the next day, over and over for months. The chronic lack of sleep affected not just my alertness, but my mood, my clarity of thinking, and my memory. I waded through mental fog every day.

"Sleep when the baby sleeps" was written as helpful advice on slips of paper by women who attended my baby shower, but I started to resent it. The phrase seemed too trite for the problem at hand, as if to say, "You'll feel fine if you just take a nap!" Occasionally, I could nap during the day when my baby did. But usually by the time I got my son to sleep, I felt keyed up. My mind was running, and it was the *only* available time to myself to do something I needed or wanted. The dishes, a bathroom break, a phone call, a shower—they all competed with sleep. I felt a sense of surrender. A nap wouldn't be enough rest to help this feeling of absolute exhaustion anyway, so what was the point?

The real problem was I didn't know what I actually needed to do to improve my sleep or how to give myself permission to rest. Naps may be a part of the solution, but women could benefit from a better understanding of the impact of sleep changes in new motherhood so it can be prioritized and a toolbox of strategies to manage it.

THE REFRAME: IT'S MORE THAN NAPS

Because babies are on a twenty-four-hour clock, so are you, and your sleep will likely be disrupted in a new and profound way. An understanding of the impact of disrupted sleep and an individualized approach to your sleep management is far more useful than a generalization about naps.

THE SCIENCE OF POSTPARTUM SLEEP

Why is sleep so important? Victoria Sharma, MD, a board-certified sleep medicine physician and medical director of a sleep disorders center, shared her insight with me. "Physiologically, sleep is vital to life. If you don't sleep, it's kind of like not eating," she said. "Sleep deprivation of twenty-four hours is actually equivalent to a blood alcohol level of 0.1—above the legal driving limit."

Dr. Sharma named a number of factors that change with lack of sleep: decreased cognitive and motor function, memory formation, alertness, and concentration; increased risk of accidents, depression, anxiety, stress, and high blood pressure; activation of the sympathetic nervous system and changes in hormone balance, such as cortisol, the hormone regulating stress response, metabolism, and inflammation. In short, "Sleep deprivation can really mess with you," she said. No wonder it feels so awful when you don't get sleep!

The normal amount of sleep needed is between six to ten hours per day, with most people needing seven to eight hours, according to Dr. Sharma. I asked if some people cope with lack of sleep better than others, and she suggested they may have a genetic predisposition. "Some people are more okay with a degree of sleep deprivation and also a change of the timing of sleep, your circadian rhythm. There are people who work night shifts, do great sleeping during the day, and then they switch back and forth and they seem fine. Others just can't handle it."

The best strategy for managing sleep for new moms is a stretch of quality sleep without disruption. Sleep cycles through stages, with a lighter stage one and two first, then deep sleep in stage three, and finally rapid eye movement (or REM) sleep. Stage three and REM sleep are more restorative and critical to physical recovery and cognitive function. When you wake to feed your baby or have a "micro-arousal" from a baby rustling or whimpering in the night, it may start the sleep cycle over at stage one—and this is what really makes mothers fatigued. Many new moms can actually manage to get a total number of hours of sleep within the normal range, but this poor sleep quality and fragmentation makes their sleep less refreshing.

Trying for consolidated, quality sleep should come first because brief naps are unlikely to make up for the fatigue from fragmented sleep (Montgomery-Downs et al. 2010, 465. e1–7). The next best strategy is increasing the total amount of sleep in any way possible (such as napping when your baby does).

TO SUMMARIZE:

1. Disrupted sleep creates physiological changes that affect our health and functioning—and can just feel awful.

2. Some people are more sensitive to sleep disruption than others.

3. Consolidated (longer) sleep is more restorative than brief naps to recover from fragmented sleep, but naps help as a second line of defense.

CAN MY BABY JUST SLEEP MORE?

The solution to sleep disruption might seem obvious: get baby to sleep more at night! There are plenty of books and theories promising to deliver this result, but it's not so straightforward for every family. Babies typically don't develop the ability to sleep through the night until six to twelve months, with plenty of individual variability (Pennestri et al. 2018). I interviewed Jen Varela, a certified gentle sleep coach and co-author of the book *Loved to Sleep,* to learn more.

Varela became interested in sleep after her own experience of new motherhood. "I had this FOMO baby who could push through his sleeping needs because he was so engaged, and he would get funnier and happier. He didn't give sleepy signals." But even if her baby didn't seem to need sleep, Varela did. "I had postpartum depression and anxiety and a little bit of obsession… I realized when I got a good chunk of sleep, like a five-hour stretch, it changed things for me." She now tells her sleep coaching clients, "You don't have to choose between loving your baby and getting the sleep you need."

How easily a baby sleeps and how compliant they will be with sleep scheduling and training (strategies to get baby to fall asleep without assistance and through the night) is largely based on the temperament they are born with and has less to do with our approach as parents. Many parents wish for a predictable schedule for their babies, but baby may not be ready or willing. In addition, "Six months is where the research shows the efforts to do sleep shaping have a long-term benefit. So, you can do some sleep shaping prior to six months, but if you're really looking at any sleep coaching or training, it's after six months," said Varela.

So how can we maximize sleep for young babies? Start with establishing attachment and good feeds. Secure attachment with primary caregivers is offered by being responsive, warm, and loving—essentially showing the baby they are safe and their needs will be met. "When a little one is not feeling safe and secure, they become hypervigilant. Your baby's actually going to get better sleep when they are in a relaxed, secure, open mindset." Down the road, babies may also be more receptive to sleep shaping strategies if a baseline of security is established.

A second strategy for maximizing babies' sleep is to prevent overtiredness, so they fall asleep more easily and sleep well when given the opportunity.

"Babies' sleep during the day is all over the place. A twenty-minute nap, a two-hour nap, a forty-five-minute nap. You really can't control how long they are going to sleep. However, the brain organizes how long they can be awake before they get overtired," said Varela.

Newborns can be awake for about an hour before overtiredness sets in. This window shifts to ninety minutes around six to eight weeks, and two to two and a half hours at six months of age. If a baby is awake beyond the appropriate window for their age, they become overtired, and cortisol kicks in. Cortisol is the stress hormone that gives them a second wind and suppresses melatonin, which promotes sleep. This makes it more difficult for your baby to fall asleep. When your baby wakes, note the time and try to get them back to sleep before their window expires.

If it seems like every parent around you is able to get their baby to sleep through the night, or nap on a schedule, "it's probably temperament," Varela said.

At around six months, however, babies are more primed for sleep shaping, such as falling asleep independently. "The awake window is longer and now you have enough time to work on a new skill without getting the cortisol surge. They're starting to consolidate some sleep cycles, getting a little more predictable schedule. The brain has shifted to being able to build more adenosine, which helps with sleep drive. So, you can go longer windows, and then you get longer naps so then they're not so overtired."

In the meantime, "rallying the troops is really key" to help parents get more sleep at night by getting assistance from a partner, family member, support person, or hired help at night.

"Research shows that the first part of the night is really where your best bang for your buck is," in terms of sleep consolidation for parents. "If Mom can go to bed as early as possible and sleep through at least the first part of the night," this can help with fatigue from sleep disruption. Bedtime is prime to introduce help from a nongestational parent or support person, when babies have the most "sleep pressure." That way, the baby is more familiar with the person who steps in to help at night wakings.

"You can't do anything to spoil or break your baby or create bad habits in the first six months of life that cannot be addressed at six months in an efficient way. So it's not worth feeling like you're always messing up or behind. So long as it's safe, and it's working, and you're getting your baby to sleep, and you're enjoying your baby, and the attachment is good. It's all good," said Varela. "Parental intuition trumps any sleep plan, any sleep book, any sleep consultant. It is the best tool parents have."

WORKING AROUND BARRIERS TO SLEEP

Many barriers can seem to block us off from getting help or lock us into existing strategies when it comes to sleep disruption. These are common barriers with offerings to increase quality sleep:

- **Breastfeeding**: When you are the source of your baby's food, it may feel like all responsibility falls on you to wake up with the baby in the night. These available strategies might help with sleep:
    - *Assistance with night feedings*: Even if you are responsible for feeding, you may be able to reduce the time you are awake in the night by allowing another person to change and/or burp the baby, return the baby to sleep, or monitor the baby's waking while you get sleep.
    - *Bottle feed with pumped milk*: You can try building a supply of milk to offer during a night awakening by pumping at a consistent time between feedings or pumping excess milk following a feeding during your waking hours. When you are ready to introduce a bottle, you can experiment with using this supply at night by having a partner or support person bottle

feed the baby. Some moms find pumping in the night is more efficient and less disruptive to sleep than feeding the baby directly if someone else can feed the baby separately and clean up pump parts.

  ○ *Supplement with formula*: Some families use a hybrid approach of using formula part of the time, such as at night, and breastfeeding the rest of the time. This allows another person to be able to help with feeding at night.

- **Light sleepers**: If you are easily roused from sleep by sounds, movements, and lights, try reducing stimulation at night:
  ○ *Sleep separately*: Sleep in a different room than baby, even if for just one segment of the night, or once a week to give yourself uninterrupted sleep. Make the room dark, use an eye mask, turn on a sound machine or app, and use earplugs to reduce outside noise if needed.
  ○ *Consolidated day sleep*: If you are not able to sleep well at night, try for a consolidated stretch of sleep during the day, such as in the morning after a feeding, with a support person looking after baby so you can turn your mind off and rest. Make your sleeping area dark, comfortable, and quiet.

- **Difficulty returning to sleep**: Consider these options if you have trouble getting back to sleep once you are awake:
  ○ *Sleep nearby*: Some moms find it is easier to feed baby overnight while co-sleeping or feeding side-lying in bed instead of getting up with the baby and creating more physical stimulation around feeding. Note the

risks of co-sleeping: You will need to evaluate if this is right for your family.

- *Decrease stimulation*: Keep lights low or off, reduce the amount of moving around that may wake your body, avoid screens or reading stimulating content while feeding at night, or use low-light settings on your device.
- *Prime your body*: Try promoting relaxation in your body to prepare for sleep through deep breathing, meditation, or progressive muscle relaxation (relaxing the muscle groups in sequence throughout your body). Many apps are available with prompts. Gentle movement during the day may also promote better sleep.
- *Prime your mind*: If thoughts keep you awake, give them a parking lot by writing them down in a journal or making a note in your phone. Try one of the relaxation techniques above to break the rumination cycle.

- **Sleep procrastination**: With the drastic shift in schedule and available free time, it is alluring to put off sleep to claim time for yourself. But if quality sleep is sacrificed for this time, the consequence will be feeling even more exhausted.
  - *Carve out time*: Make time during waking hours for pleasurable activities such as during one of your baby's naps or asking a support person to watch your baby while you engage in something essential or enjoyable.
  - *Alternate you time and sleep time*: Schedule in nights when you allow yourself to stay up for a show or connection with your partner and alternate them with nights you turn in early to get consolidated sleep.

- **Mental health**: Mental health disorders such as anxiety, depression, PTSD, and OCD can compound sleep disruption with symptoms such as difficulty falling and staying asleep, waking in the night, disruptive thoughts, and nightmares.
    - *Seek treatment*: Reach out to a therapist, support group, OBGYN, or primary care doctor to get support if you have untreated mental health concerns. See chapter eight for more information about postpartum mental health. When symptoms are reduced, sleep may improve. If you are unable to sleep even when given the opportunity, contact your OBGYN, primary care doctor, therapist, or psychiatrist right away for help.

ADDITIONAL RESOURCES FOR SLEEP

- Get creative in finding support by asking family members or trusted friends to help with stretches of time to sleep. Do you know anyone who is a natural night owl? Can someone help while you sleep during the day? Could you open a fund for hired support in lieu of baby shower gifts?
- Several types of professionals are available for hire to help with sleep support:
    - At night:
        - Night doula
        - Night nanny
        - Baby nurse
    - During the day:
        - Mother's helper
        - Babysitter
        - Doula
        - Nanny

- Talk to a sleep coach or consultant if you have questions about improving baby's sleep or would like to start sleep training.
- Protect your boundaries and wind-down rituals around sleep to make the most of your available sleep time. Create a quiet and comfortable sleep space, avoid caffeine and alcohol before bed, and put screens down before sleep. Delegate or take things off your plate to make time for sleeping.

SLEEP STRATEGIES FROM OTHER MOMS

"My husband would change the diapers in the night, I would feed, then when the baby woke up around 6:00 a.m., he would take her downstairs and I'd sleep until the next feeding."

—HEATHER D.

"For our second child I decided to sleep in her bedroom on a blow-up mattress. I slept more when she slept, and it made getting to her in the night easier."

—ANONYMOUS, CALIFORNIA

"Co-sleeping."

—ANELISE H.

"Formula feeding at night."

—ANONYMOUS, ILLINOIS

"Moving baby to their own room at five weeks."

—JENNA

"Once a week, going to the spare bedroom after the 11:00 p.m. nursing and my husband sleeping with the baby until they woke to nurse."

—LORI F.

"Switching off sleep-in mornings with my partner."

—AMY

"A night nanny once a week, getting mother-in-law's help, sleeping in separate rooms."

—ANONYMOUS, MASSACHUSETTS

"Turn off the monitor."

—ANONYMOUS, ARIZONA

"Canceling plans. If I wasn't getting sleep, I couldn't be present for other activities. We need to quit trying to show up for everyone when we need to show up for our families and ourselves first."

—MADDIE

EXERCISES FOR REFRAMING

KNOW YOUR SLEEP PROFILE

Review the questions below to take an honest assessment of what your needs are around sleep so you know which steps and strategies will be helpful.

Ask someone who knows you well, such as a partner, family member, or close friend, to give their impressions on your sleep profile to help fill in your picture. Discuss your profile together with your partner, if applicable, to get a sense of both of your needs around sleep changes.

How do you typically cope when you miss a good night's sleep? Terrible? Just fine? If you are already postpartum, how are you doing with the sleep changes?

Are you a light sleeper (i.e., wake easily to sounds, movements, or light)?

Do you have trouble returning to sleep if awakened in the night?

Do you procrastinate or de-prioritize sleep?

MAKE A SLEEP GAME PLAN

Based on your sleep profile above, identify what support you need to get more sleep now or what you would like to line up when your baby arrives.

WAYS TO WORK IT IN

Brainstorm with your partner or a friend, family member, or support person to get clear on what your needs are and the ways to meet them. Work with a professional such as a night doula to develop a plan.

When you review your sleep profile, where is it clear you need support?

What resources from this chapter are you willing to experiment with to meet your sleep needs (such as a "shift" of sleep in a separate room from baby, a sound machine, hiring help, etc.)?

Do you and your partner need a system to ensure good sleep for both of you? What would support this?

Would you like to make any shifts to make sleep a higher priority (for example, no watching TV before bed, delegating the dinner dishes so you can get to sleep earlier, etc.)?

What are three steps you can take for better sleep?

1. The effect of sleep disruption in new motherhood is often a shock because chronically fragmented sleep can alter your functioning in a way you may have never experienced.
2. Infants typically do not have the ability to sleep through the night until six to twelve months of age. Establishing secure attachment with your baby and timing sleep to prevent overtiredness may improve sleep in early months, but there is no magic solution to get babies to sleep on cue or overnight until they are ready.
3. Consolidated (longer, uninterrupted) stretches of sleep work best against sleep disruption fatigue. Ways to achieve this include arranging support with a partner, family member, or hired professional and using strategies to make waking less disruptive, return to sleep easier, and sleep a priority. Assessing your sleep profile can highlight where to add support.

Sleep disruption can be one of the most challenging aspects of new parenthood, and it may take some trial and error to find the right strategies to support you. But the opportunity to improve your sleep and feel better is worth the effort. One day, your child will sleep through the night, and this will get easier. I promise.

In the next chapter, we will examine the pressures of "having it all" and the consequences of our attachment to this myth.

MOTHERHOOD MYTH #7:
YOU CAN HAVE IT ALL

She has it all: a career she's worked hard for, two and a half adorable kids, and a neatly manicured house with a white picket fence. When she's not volunteering in her child's classroom, you can find her staying fit in Pilates class while tonight's dinner simmers in the Crockpot. It's the super-mom ideal at the heart of modern motherhood: women can balance career, family, and basically everything else. It sounds good, but how is it really going?

In the process of Western feminist liberation, we were given the green light to work instead of just being confined to the home. Yet the infrastructure to support women in this shift and a re-balancing of home workload has not kept up. Mothers *do* have it all—but in a system that values their time less than men's and without the support to make it sustainable.

In the US, paid family leave is not standardized and childcare is limited and expensive, creating barriers for working mothers. While other countries view paid leave as an aspect of public health care, at the time of this writing, the United States is one of just a handful of countries in the world without national paid leave. Eighty percent of US workers have no paid time off after the birth or adoption of a child (Coombs 2021, 1). In addition, childcare "has become an increasingly crushing expense for families with young children. Over the past two decades, the cost of childcare has more than doubled, while wages have remained mostly stagnant. Many parents find childcare expenses consume most of their paycheck, and some decide to leave the workforce as a result" (Schochet 2019, 6).

Women's pay is still not equivalent to men's and is hit with a "motherhood penalty" that decreases women's wages by 4 percent per child, on average. Lower-wage working women are penalized even more. Men get a "bonus" of an average 6 percent *increase* in pay when they become fathers. These trends are found across a number of Westernized countries (but improve with publicly funded childcare for young children). Employers may also discriminate against mothers in callbacks for job applications, hiring decisions, wage offers, and promotions (Budig 2014, 9-23).

At home, women tend to be the "shefault" parent for more than their share of household tasks, as Eve Rodsky describes in her book *Fair Play* (2019, 7). Globally, women spend nearly 2.5 hours more per day in "unpaid labor" compared to men (OECD 2023). American women in opposite-sex partnered relationships do a greater amount of household work and have less leisure time than men, even when women make similar or *more* income than their partners. Only when women are the sole adult employed in a household do men pitch in more than women (Fry, Aragao, Hurst, and Parker 2023, 4–5). In same-sex relationships, this time is typically divided more equally, but partners who make less income usually do more household and caregiving tasks once they become parents (Cain Miller 2018).

Women also do more of the "cognitive labor" of managing a household, such as anticipating needs, identifying options for filling them, and monitoring progress of completion (Daminger 2019, 609). So, if the diapers or formula are running low, it's more likely a mom will notice, plan replenishment, and make sure it's done. These mental tasks are typically undervalued because they are invisible yet cost women time and energy to keep them constantly running.

If we peel back more layers of having it all, we find additional pressures on moms: how your home looks (tidy and decorated), how your body looks (slim and beautiful), how you feed your family (organic and made from scratch), your relationship status (blissful partnership)—and all of it should look social media worthy.

It's a lopsided and dysfunctional system that places immense pressure on mothers.

You might be thinking, "But Andrea, I still like the idea of having it all!" That's okay. The problem is expecting satisfaction under these pressures and perfection being what we all aspire to. When the bar is set so high and without adequate support, we risk burning ourselves out and stigmatizing the women who become overwhelmed by this undertaking—and believe me, they're out there. I saw it in the clients coming to my office. I see it as harried moms drop off children at our school or are breaking down in their car in the preschool parking lot. I witness my friends constantly seeking balance between caring for themselves, their families, and their professional responsibilities. I am still figuring it out.

Do we keep running on the motherhood treadmill and striving to fit the expectation, or do we listen to our needs and define our own experience? Nobody gets a trophy for doing things in the hardest or most perfect way. Here's what I propose: slow down, reassess, and do enough.

THE REFRAME: YOU CAN DO ENOUGH

When "having it all" is dictated by a mythical expectation that we should be able to do everything, flawlessly, all the time, it is a setup for failure and guilt. The risk is erosion of our self-esteem and deterioration of our physical and mental health—a recipe for burnout. "Doing enough" is an alternative that allows us to set our own standards.

JOY'S STORY

Joy reached out to me to share her matrescence story. She's an Asian American mother with hip style and four young children. Our conversation centered around the balance of doing enough and the complexity of having it all. She was so generous with her honesty. We met at a coffee shop, and her phone buzzed with texts from her babysitter while we talked.

"I am a great mom, but at the same time, I feel like I could be doing more. I don't know if I *need* to be doing more. That's the thing," she said. "Am I doing my kids wrong by not enforcing their full homework schedule, or because we're going out to eat at McDonald's? I think about these little nuances daily."

Joy owns a part-time yoga business and recently added a full-time job. When working part time, she wished for more socialization with adults. She told her husband, "There's something missing. Maybe I need to do more work. And then as I slowly put in more effort to working, I felt there was this push of 'Gosh, do my kids need me?'"

When I asked where these pressures come from, she reflected on how hard her parents worked and how she wants to provide a better life for her children than she had growing up. "Then you see Rihanna," referring to the star's Super Bowl Half Time performance while pregnant. "All these thoughts came into my head like, well, if she can do it, then I can too. But then I realized, I'm not a celebrity. That's not my job description. So why should I try to live up to that or live up to what I see on social media?" It took time for Joy to affirm external images are not how she has to live her life as a mom. "I needed to stop the scrolling."

She summarized the push and pull of having it all. "You're trying to find what the end goal is. So you just keep achieving, achieving, achieving, not knowing where your limit is… And then even though I tell myself, 'Hey, you can't do it all. Why are you doing it all?' I don't have an answer. I just *want* to do it all. So that might be something I need to reflect on. What are you doing to yourself and where are you going?" She acknowledged there is no perfect version of motherhood. "It's going to be *your* version of perfect and *your* version of balance. I think that's one thing I was striving for is balance. I need to be accepting of the balance that works for me."

Joy's reflections describe the condition of modern motherhood and having it all. Many mothers are conforming to ideals, pushing to their limits, but wondering about the end goal and if the process is fulfilling. The answers Joy seeks are evasive for many moms. To really see them, we need to pause and intentionally define the limits for ourselves.

DEFINING "ENOUGH"

No one has infinite time or energy, yet this is where the bar is set with having it all. In contrast, doing enough sets a healthy boundary around your time and energy, as well as your expectations for yourself. To have limits is normal, and acknowledging them breaks the cycle of limitless expectations and constant shortcomings.

What is "enough"? It depends on how you want your life to look and feel. Each area of your life requires some of your limited store of energy: a career, partnership, raising a child, pursuing interests and goals, maintaining a home, and so on. Not all areas of your life can have 100 percent of your focus at all times because that requires more energy than you have available.

You will find a child naturally draws lots of your energy because they rely on caregivers for so much of what they need—especially babies. This limits the capacity for the rest of your responsibilities and interests. If you identify what is most important to get out of your life, you can align your energy with those things to derive the most meaning and satisfaction from your time.

To develop your unique mix of "enough," take stock of what is most important, energizing, and essential in your life. The rest can be outsourced or downsized. Some things will need to be let go.

If the idea of letting go makes your heart skip a beat, imagine this as a process of tending your life garden. To make space for new growth, some areas will need pruning and weeding. Sometimes you will feel satisfaction and relief for how things are rearranged. Other times, you will grieve what used to be. Notice how you feel and honor your needs. Take time to step back and admire, and re-work the areas that still seem off-kilter. The exercises at the end of this chapter will provide guidance.

DIALING UP SUPPORT

What about the parts of life that genuinely require your attention, but you don't have enough time and energy to get it all done? It's time for help. This could be with dinner, shopping, transporting kids, childcare, housework, or errands—you name it. Instead of expecting ourselves to "do it all," we need to dial up support for the essential areas to get accomplished.

When I asked Dawn Dickerson, lactation consultant and parent educator, about calling in help, she said, "In our society we have this huge pressure of doing it alone. And that is the greatest problem: people think that in order to achieve whatever 'success' is in their head, that they have to do it on their own." She sees asking for help as a uniquely human asset, starting from the very beginning with a baby's ability to cry. They remind us how we are social and interconnected creatures and how asking for help is a key strategy to survive.

Visit chapter four for a refresher on calling in help. It doesn't have to be fancy or expensive. Chapter ten will offer tips for dividing and negotiating tasks with a partner. Start practicing the art of asking and supporting yourself right from the beginning, when your baby arrives.

ENCOUNTERS WITH OUTSIDE EXPECTATIONS

Developing our own definition of "enough" involves contending with outside views about motherhood and how our lives should look from our family, peers, and society. Cue judgmental voices: If you work, what about your children? If you stay at home, why not work? And what are you making for dinner? Well *that* won't help you lose your baby weight…

One mom shared:

> *"I'm a homeschooling stay-at-home mom and I literally feel like I'm invisible to the general public in social interactions. When I tell a room full of people what I 'do' they suddenly cease to have any interest in speaking to me."*
>
> —CATHARINA G.

While the world catches up to understand the value of doing enough, two things may help:

1. *Write your own script*: Get grounded in what you believe is true for yourself and your life. When you make it clear what matters to you, others may be less compelled to fill in the blanks about how they think you should conduct your life. It may even spark interest. If judgment still comes, you can be prepared with what to say and continue to stick to the script. An exercise at the end of the chapter will walk you through this.

2. *Create boundaries*: Protect yourself against sources of judgment. If you have a judgmental or advice-giving person, group, or organization in your life, build in barriers to look after yourself. It could be limiting time spent with them, layering in another person who has your back when they are around, having some diffusing statements on hand, like "I'll consider that when I'm ready," or telling them directly you are finding your own way as a new mother and will ask for guidance when you need it. Dickerson suggests to her clients to keep a notebook handy for advice. When advice is offered, say, "I'm exhausted. I really want to hear what you have to say, and I know I'm not going to remember it. Please write it down for me." Then you can read it if you choose—or not.

EXERCISES FOR REFRAMING

ASSESS WHAT REALLY MATTERS

Take stock of what is most important in how you live your life by answering the questions below. Find a few quiet minutes for reflection, so you can slow down and ask: What do I really want?

Take fifteen to twenty minutes to answer these questions while your baby naps or a trusted person watches your baby. Walk your baby in a stroller or carrier to contemplate your answers. Dictate your answers into your phone if it's easier. Discuss with a friend, partner, family member, or therapist if you get stuck or want to process.

Before you answer these questions, deepen your mindset by imagining there is a direct connection from your soul to this page to channel your answers.

How do you want to experience your life? How would you like it to look and feel? What do you really want?

What is essential in your life—the things you must do?

What is optional in your life—the things you can do?

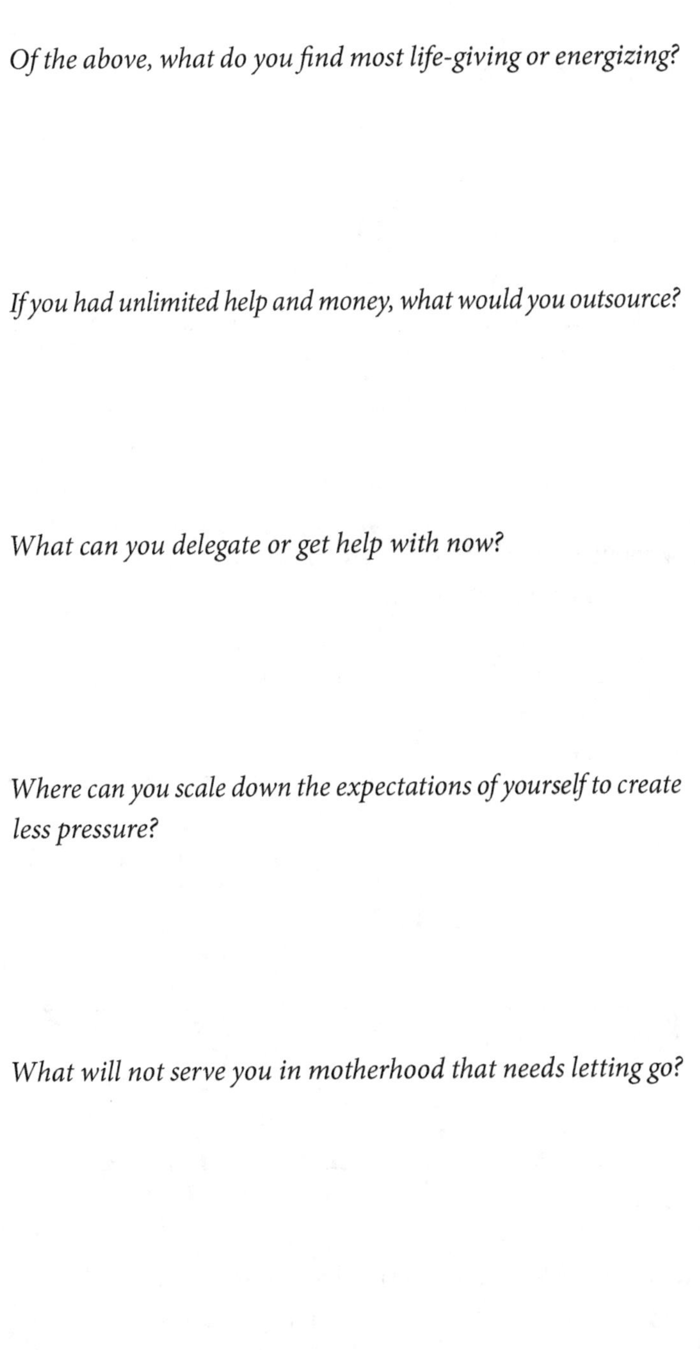

Of the above, what do you find most life-giving or energizing?

If you had unlimited help and money, what would you outsource?

What can you delegate or get help with now?

Where can you scale down the expectations of yourself to create less pressure?

What will not serve you in motherhood that needs letting go?

Permission Slip for Letting Go:

I, ____,
give myself permission to let go of

____

____

______________________________________,

without guilt or shame, because it:
- Does not serve me in motherhood
- Is unnecessary
- Is an ideal I don't need to live up to
- Is not a priority right now, but I'd like to come back to it later

- Other: _________________________

____

____

Signed: _________________________

Date: _________________________

Perhaps you'd even like a ritual to commemorate the letting go. Consider burning, tearing up, giving or casting away, burying, wrapping sacredly, having a party, or saying words to the wind. This could be done alone or in the company of others. What do you need to honor your letting go process?

WRITE YOUR SCRIPT

The purpose of this script is to consolidate what you revealed in the previous exercise and clarify the narrative about your life. This can be for your benefit only or to present to your external world.

WAYS TO WORK IT IN

Read your script out loud with a friend, partner, or your baby. Keep it in your phone to practice or revise. Notice how it feels to you if you change it up. Get feedback, if you like, from a trusted source.

Develop your own way of describing your life structure, encompassing the parts that are important to you. You may find different wording elicits different engagement or a perspective shift, such as "I'm CEO of the Household" or "chief kid officer" versus "I'm a stay-at-home mom." Describe the important parts of how you structure (or wish to structure) your life:

Include what you are doing, rather than focusing on what you are not. Would you like to lead with your profession? Are there hobbies, projects, passions, side hustles, or volunteering you would prefer to lead with? For example, "I __________ (hobbies, projects, volunteering) when I'm not home with my baby," or "I work as __________, but my real passion is __________."

Identify how your life structure works for you. How does it relate to what you value in life? You could say, "It works really well for us to live a balanced life," "I appreciate this opportunity to spend time with my kids," or "I love my career. I feel I am truly making a difference in the world."

Add a time frame, if relevant. Is it permanent, temporary, or fluid? "This works for me right now," or "I used to __________ (occupation/activity). I'll return to it when I am ready."

Bring it together in a statement you can get grounded in. You don't have to explain yourself or your choices, just state them as facts. This may take a couple drafts and a few tries to find the right fit. You may need to repeat parts of your script to decrease advice-giving or questioning by restating a main point, such as, "It works really well for us right now."

TAKEAWAYS

1. "Having it all" is embedded in the dream of modern motherhood but has shifted from an opportunity to an expectation for mothers to excel at everything, all the time, in a system providing inadequate support.

2. Instead of chasing boundless expectations, we can "do enough" and create our own definition of what we want in our lives and set limits.

3. Taking stock of what is most important to us, letting go of what is not, dialing up support, and having a clear narrative when faced with outside expectations can help in the transition to building a life aligned with your *own* needs instead of societal expectations.

Creating our own version of "enough" is a courageous and daring act. It is also freeing. Releasing the pressures of performing to a shifting and sky-high standard makes space to embrace the life you want to live. Experiment with your version of doing enough, and notice how it works for you.

The next chapter explores mental health during pregnancy and postpartum. Mental health challenges are the number one medical complication of childbirth, and this topic deserves our attention, even if it feels uncomfortable to acknowledge.

MOTHERHOOD MYTH #8:

IT'S THE HAPPIEST TIME

———

In the weeks after I had my son, something wasn't right. I could tell but desperately didn't want to acknowledge it because that seemed like a failure as a mother. I felt deeply sad, trapped, exhausted, like I wasn't good at parenthood, keyed up, and like I wanted to escape. But this wasn't how I thought I should feel.

I should be loving motherhood. It should be the happiest time of my life. This was the predominant message I received about motherhood, and it's what I *thought* I saw when I looked around at other mothers. So, I tried to hold it together. I put the added pressure on myself of questioning how I could go back to being a therapist after maternity leave if I needed mental health help myself.

When I had my six-week postpartum checkup, I slid under the radar. I looked okay, I said I was okay, and my provider couldn't know what I was really experiencing. It was my son's pediatrician who casually questioned and lowered the barrier for me to open up.

The doctor asked as he examined my baby, "So, how are you doing?"

"I'm doing fine. I have my down days, but I'm okay," I said.

"Down days. What does that mean?" he asked.

"I don't know. I guess I just feel overwhelmed and sad sometimes."

He then asked who was helping me with the baby (no one except my husband when he came home from work) and what my days looked like. In a warm but direct tone, he said, "You're spending too much time with the baby. You need help so you can take breaks."

At the time I heard those words, it was groundbreaking. He was the first person to convey a new message: prioritize taking care of yourself. You're not crazy if you don't love every moment of time with your baby, especially with few breaks. He normalized my experience of this not being the happiest time, and to hear this from the doctor whose primary interest was my son felt so validating. This was a turning point in shifting away from thinking I had to hold it all together to avoid shame and tolerating the vulnerability of admitting I had postpartum depression and anxiety and needed help.

Shame and stigma are powerful. They can keep our stories from being told, our truths from being acknowledged, and hold us in the darkness. Mental health issues have long been stigmatized, and maternal mental health is no exception. To acknowledge its existence is in opposition to the dominant cultural message that motherhood is a blissful, happy time. There has also been a lack of information about the breadth and prevalence of mental health issues during pregnancy and postpartum. To make matters worse, media representation has often been of extreme cases, sensationalized, and incorrectly represented as the full picture of what maternal mental health looks like.

Mothers face incredible barriers to speak up about mental health and mobilize help: the lack of information about maternal mental health risks and disorders; the fear of being labeled as "crazy" or outside the norm for admitting they are struggling, or worse, they will be perceived as incapable of taking care of their children. But there's a huge cost to this system of silence: mothers suffering when they could be getting well. Not only does this steal the joy from new motherhood, but when mothers feel awful, it affects the whole family system, from baby bonding and care to partner relationships.

Here's the real scoop on maternal mental health: Approximately one in five women will have a mental health disorder during pregnancy or postpartum, defined as the year after having a baby. Postpartum depression affects over five hundred thousand women per year in the US alone, making mental health disorders one of the most common complications of childbirth. Despite being a time of elevated risk, these disorders are frequently under detected and under treated (Van Niel and Payne 2020, 273–274).

We now understand there are a variety of mental health experiences during pregnancy and postpartum called perinatal mood and anxiety disorders (PMAD). These can affect mothers of any age, race, ethnicity, or income level (Postpartum Support International 2015). PMAD are *treatable* conditions, making it even more important women reach out for help, because recovery is possible and can be like adding color again to a life that slipped into black and white.

I take heart in seeing recent advances in education and understanding of maternal mental health. I've been proud to be a part of developing this in my local community. But I believe we should not slow down until education about maternal mental health becomes a standard part of care for all mothers, and every mom knows: Having a baby creates a unique window for mental health, when we should be especially attuned to how we are *honestly* doing.

THE REFRAME: NEW MOTHERHOOD IS A VULNERABLE TIME FOR MENTAL HEALTH

Shame and stigma often prevent moms from talking about their mental health in pregnancy and postpartum, when it's supposed to be "the happiest time of life." But all the transition, sleep changes, and hormone fluctuations make it an obvious time of mental health vulnerability. The more we can talk about maternal mental health, the more we can understand mothers are not to blame for mental health disorders, and treatment is possible and critical.

WHY IS IT A VULNERABLE TIME?

Significant life transitions are typically a risk factor for mental health vulnerability. Moving, loss, divorce, a pandemic, a new school—all of these could trigger a mental health event.

Matrescence, even if a welcome and positive life change, is still a significant transition touching many facets of life. Mix this with the sleep deprivation and hormonal changes common in new motherhood (that can *also* create mental health problems all on their own), and the mental health risk in pregnancy and postpartum becomes clear.

This doesn't doom all mothers to have mental illness during pregnancy or postpartum, but it normalizes the experience for the one in five women who do. Awareness of symptoms empowers mothers to make more immediate connections with their mental health experiences and engage help. Mental health is treatable. Mothers can feel better. But only if conditions are recognized and treatment is sought.

Specific situations and populations increase the risk for mental health disorders, including:

- Personal history of mental health disorders
- Family history of mental health disorders
- Unwanted or teen pregnancy
- Mothers of multiples
- Traumatic birth or pregnancy
- Health challenges for baby or preterm birth
- Lack of support
- Substance abuse
- Sensitivity to changes in reproductive hormones (such as PMS or when using hormonal birth control)
- Native American or Native Hawaiian women (Van Niel and Payne 2020, 274)
- Hispanic women
- Black women (Mukherjee et al. 2016, 1780)

- History of physical, psychological, or sexual abuse
- Intimate partner violence
- Women who experience discrimination
- Women who are immigrants
- Women experiencing other stressors, such as financial problems, divorce, recent loss, or natural disaster
- Low income or low education (Guintivano, Manuck, and Meltzer-Brody 2018, 591-601)
- Active-duty women in the military
- Military spouses, especially around military deployment (Klaman and Turner 2016, S63)

WHAT DO DISORDERS LOOK LIKE?

"Postpartum depression" used to be the catch-all phrase for what we now call PMAD, a broader range of mental health experiences including perinatal depression, anxiety, obsessive-compulsive disorder, post-traumatic stress disorder, bipolar disorder, and postpartum psychosis. "Perinatal" means "around birth." Disorders may start any time during the period from pregnancy through the first year after having a baby. Some women will have more than one disorder at the same time, such as depression and anxiety together.

The following is a breakdown of what PMAD look like during pregnancy and postpartum. Only a medical or mental health professional can diagnose these disorders, but anyone can build an understanding of them and advocate for their assessment and treatment. Please, seek help from a medical doctor, therapist, or psychiatrist if you think you are suffering from any of these disorders. See the Getting Well section later in this chapter for more information about treatment options, and the resources section at the back of the book is a good quick guide.

I'd like to acknowledge you might not feel like reading this section. No one wants mental health issues as a part of their journey of motherhood, and we can feel an aversion to even seeing or hearing the information. My promise to you is knowledge of mental health issues does not make it more likely they will affect you. This insight will make it easier to recognize and take action if you do happen to need it. Try on a perspective of curiosity as if you are gathering information for a dear friend and keep reading. You're doing great.

BABY BLUES

Baby Blues is *not* a mental health disorder but rather a cluster of symptoms up to 80 percent of birthing mothers experience in the first days postpartum. The cause is thought to be the biochemical changes in the body after delivering a baby. Symptoms are *mild and temporary*—they end within about two weeks after delivery without intervention and aren't disruptive to daily functioning (Van Niel and Payne 2020, 273).

If symptoms are severe or last beyond two weeks, this may be a sign of a more significant mental health disorder such as postpartum depression or anxiety instead (more on these below). I have heard clients or friends refer to their "baby blues" that lasted for months. This is not how baby blues should look, and it is not "a normal part of motherhood" to experience these symptoms long term. For severe or lasting symptoms, take steps to feel better (see the Getting Well section below).

Symptoms of baby blues include feeling:

- Tearful/weepy
- Drained
- Uncertainty
- Mildly anxious or sad
- Overwhelmed
- Irritable
- Emotional ups and downs

PERINATAL DEPRESSION

Up to 20 percent of women will experience perinatal depression, starting any time from pregnancy through the first year after birth (Van Niel and Payne 2020, 273). Most often, depression is experienced as a mood of sadness or emptiness. It can also present as agitation, irritability, or anger. Sometimes it involves thoughts of suicide or wishing to "go away," but this is not a requirement.

Depression can be invisible. Many of the women who walked into my office seeking help postpartum looked put together, and I wouldn't have worried about them if we passed on the street as strangers. Only until they shared the depth of their internal experience was the depression apparent. If depression symptoms become disruptive to your everyday life or last two weeks or more, reach out to a professional immediately (see the Getting Well section below). You don't have to suffer in silence.

Symptoms of depression include:

- Primary mood is sadness and/or irritability/anger
- Frequent crying

- Unable to sleep when given the opportunity, waking early, or wanting to oversleep
- Undereating or overeating
- Lack of interest in things usually pleasurable
- Feeling "blank," empty, or lack of emotion
- Feeling weighed down or in slow motion
- Problems with everyday functioning such as taking care of self or baby
- Hopelessness
- Self-esteem is low, sense of worthlessness
- Excessive guilt
- Thinking about hurting or killing self, wishing to not exist anymore
- "This doesn't feel like me"

"I had postpartum depression after my first baby. I really thought those first weeks would be so joyous, and I just felt like I was sinking into a pit."

—CATHARINA G.

PERINATAL ANXIETY

Up to 17 percent of postpartum women and 21 percent of women during pregnancy experience anxiety (Fairbrother et al. 2015, 2). Symptoms can begin anytime during pregnancy through the first year postpartum. Worrying about your health or your baby when you are a new mother is normal, but when these worries disrupt your day-to-day functioning, feel extreme, or last two weeks or more, talk to a professional for help managing symptoms so you can get back to the important stuff: your baby and matrescence.

Symptoms of anxiety include:

- Feeling agitated, irritable, or restless
- Feeling nervous, on alert, or like something bad is going to happen
- Racing thoughts
- Shortness of breath (like it's hard to catch your breath as though you've been exercising)
- Undereating or overeating
- Difficulty staying or falling asleep
- Excessive worry about the baby or yourself
- Physical symptoms like dizziness, hot flashes, heart beating fast, gastrointestinal problems (diarrhea, nausea, stomachache, gas, constipation)

Some women also experience panic attacks: brief, intense episodes of anxiety that happen with a trigger, or spontaneously, and may include shortness of breath, chest pain, sensation of throat closing in/choking, dizziness, trembling, rapid heart rate, numbness or tingling sensations, or feeling outside of the body. This can feel like a heart attack or as if you might be dying but usually resolves in minutes.

"There should be more discussion on postpartum anxiety. I knew I wasn't depressed but also had no clue that envisioning hundreds of ways my child could die every moment was something I could get help with. I thought it was just the way it was, or something wrong with just me."

—AMANDA H.

PERINATAL OBSESSIVE-COMPULSIVE DISORDER (OCD)

Pregnant and postpartum women are 1.5 to two times more likely to experience OCD than the general population, and women who previously had OCD are more likely to experience recurring symptoms in this time (Vladan et al. 2020, 966). OCD is characterized by recurrent thoughts or images that are difficult to control and affect the ability to function (obsessions). Common themes of thoughts are: What if I or my baby is harmed, what if *I* harm my baby, or I need to protect us from germs and illnesses? Thoughts can be graphic and disturbing to moms. They know the thoughts are unusual and typically do not have a desire to act on them.

Some women also have compulsions—behaviors that feel necessary or irresistible to reduce anxiety or threats. This might be excessively checking if the baby is breathing in the night, handwashing over and over, extreme cleaning or laundering, repetitive counting or rearranging things, or hoarding items.

Symptoms of OCD include:
- Recurrent obsessive thoughts or mental images
- Compulsive actions such as checking, counting, rearranging, cleaning
- Feeling horrified, scared, or ashamed of obsessive thoughts

- Avoidance of situations, settings, or objects related to disturbing thoughts
- Feeling on high alert
- Fear of being alone with baby because of disturbing thoughts

"I had pretty graphic and scary irrational thoughts that were intrusive and horrifying. My bedroom was on the second floor of our home and the staircase was right outside our door. I would have recurring thoughts of seeing my baby drop/fall from the stairs, and it felt like there was no way to avoid it. I experienced a lot of shame because I am educated and trained as a mental health professional, but I was in such a dense fog mentally that it was hard to even know that what I was experiencing wasn't okay. I had a harder time reaching out for help than I would like to admit and felt completely alone."

—ANONYMOUS, NASHVILLE, TENNESSEE

PERINATAL POST-TRAUMATIC STRESS DISORDER (PTSD)

When most people hear the term PTSD, they think about war veterans or disaster survivors—big and dramatic traumas. But trauma can occur in many ways and to everyday people. Our minds and bodies don't always distinguish between a "big" trauma and a smaller one and may manifest the same reaction in the body.

About 4 to 6 percent of women experience perinatal PTSD (Yildiz, Ayers, and Phillips 2017, 634–635). Perinatal PTSD could arise after events like severe pregnancy symptoms, medical complications, reactivated traumas from the past (such as a history of sexual abuse), traumatic birth, perinatal loss, or a baby in the NICU.

Symptoms of PTSD include:

- Reexperiencing a traumatic event in the mind or body with flashbacks, memories, thoughts, or dreams
- Avoiding reminders of a traumatic event, such as aversion to certain scents, sounds, objects, locations, etc.
- Startling easily
- Feeling keyed up, agitated, or on high alert
- Isolating
- Excessive sense of guilt or blame around a traumatic event
- Feeling disconnected or outside of one's body (disassociating)
- Less interest in previously enjoyed activities
- Inability to remember parts of a traumatic event

PERINATAL BIPOLAR DISORDER

Bipolar disorder is characterized by having at least one episode of mania (an unusually euphoric, energized, or agitated state) or phases of both hypomania (shorter and milder than mania) and depression. Many women get misdiagnosed with only depression who actually have bipolar disorder. Treatment approaches for depression and bipolar disorder are different, so an accurate diagnosis by a professional is important. About half of women already diagnosed with bipolar disorder will have a perinatal mood episode, and about 3 percent of moms will have bipolar disorder for the first time during pregnancy and postpartum (Masters et al. 2022, e1).

Get help right away if you think you have bipolar disorder. *Phases of mania are typically a mental health emergency because they can lead to risky behavior. Please contact your medical provider, therapist, psychiatrist, or the national crisis hotline at 9-8-8.*

Symptoms of bipolar disorder include:
- An uncharacteristically euphoric, energized, or irritable mood (mania) lasting days
- Inflated self-esteem and belief in capabilities
- Decreased need for sleep (fully energized after sleeping three to four hours or not at all)
- Pressure to talk continuously, racing thoughts
- Increased activity level
- Impulsive behaviors like excessive spending, giving away possessions, sexual promiscuity, reckless driving, or grandiose decisions
- Alternating between manic and depressed mood (sad, slowed down, empty) at the same time or in distinct phases
- Sometimes may include delusions (believing untrue things) or hallucinations (seeing or hearing things that are not real) (American Psychiatric Association 2013, 123–138)

Women with bipolar disorder are at high risk for postpartum episodes and have greater risk for experiencing postpartum psychosis, described in the next section (Wesseloo, et al. 2015, 117–126).

POSTPARTUM PSYCHOSIS

Postpartum psychosis is a rare and severe, but treatable, condition. It affects approximately one to two women per one thousand births, typically in the first weeks after delivery

(VanderKruik et al. 2017, 8). Because it can lead to bizarre and dangerous behaviors, postpartum psychosis is a mental health emergency and requires urgent attention. *Get help immediately for any of the following symptoms by calling a medical provider, psychiatrist, text/call the national crisis hotline at 9-8-8, or call 9-1-1.*

Symptoms of postpartum psychosis include:

- Bizarre thinking or behavior, strange suspicions
- Delusions (believing things that are not true) and feeling compelled to act on them
- Unable to discern reality
- Poor concentration, severely distracted
- Unable to sleep when given the opportunity
- Confusion or disorientation
- Rapid mood changes
- Excessively active or severely slowed down
- Hallucinations (seeing, hearing, or feeling things that are not real)
- Decreased ability to care for self or the baby
- Thoughts of harming self and/or the baby that seem rational to the mom (Sit, Rothschild, and Wisner 2006, 352-368)

DYSPHORIC MILK EJECTION REFLEX (D-MER)

D-MER is not a mental health disorder but a phenomenon around 9 percent of women experience during breast milk letdown. Right before or during milk letdown, D-MER causes feelings of anxiety, sadness, nervousness, irritability, nausea, chills, rapid heart rate, a hollow feeling in the stomach, or a sense of dread. This lasts for up to ten minutes and then subsides, with a normal mood all other times. The occurrence of these symptoms may subside around three months postpartum but may not go away until breastfeeding is stopped (Frawley and McGuinness 2023, 620-622). If you experience D-MER and want to continue breastfeeding, working with a lactation consultant, therapist, or pumping and bottle-feeding breast milk may be helpful for managing symptoms. Some women choose to stop breastfeeding if D-MER is highly distressing.

POSTPARTUM MENTAL HEALTH FOR DADS AND NON-BIRTHING PARENTS

Even though they are not delivering the baby, dads, adoptive parents, and nongestational parents can also experience mental health challenges postpartum. Up to one in ten new dads will experience postpartum depression, 4 percent will have postpartum anxiety, and 5 percent will have postpartum PTSD (Scarff 2019, 11).

Dr. Daniel Singley, a clinical psychologist specializing in paternal and men's issues and coauthor of *Parental Mental Health: Factoring in Fathers*, told me mental health during the transition to parenthood is "a people problem, not just a male or female problem." It's not only physical changes related to birth that create a vulnerable time for mental health after becoming a caregiver to a baby, although men have been found to experience hormonal changes during a woman's pregnancy and postpartum (Scarff 2019, 12). The changes in sleep, the changes in life, and the additional stressors related to becoming a parent can also affect mental health. Non-birthing parents, regardless of sex or gender, have an increased risk for mental health disorders, as well as adoptive parents and parents through surrogacy. The transition to parenthood can be significant for *any* parent.

This information is not an assignment to "fix" your partner if you notice they are struggling with their mental health after a baby comes into your life. Rather, it is a way to have awareness, share information, and empower them to reach out for help if they are not feeling well. Talk about the challenges you anticipate together.

GETTING WELL

If you recognize symptoms in this chapter in yourself or partner or are feeling like something is just not right with your emotional wellbeing, get help. When symptoms are not addressed, they tend to last. Both you and your baby deserve for you to be well—and this even improves health and social outcomes for your baby. You can engage support for these treatable mental health disorders in a variety of ways:

- **Individual therapy**: a licensed professional who listens, validates, and provides education and skills on a regular basis to guide you in improving your symptoms. Many providers offer online therapy since COVID-19, making therapy more accessible. Someone who is knowledgeable about PMAD, motherhood, or certified in perinatal mental health (PMH-C) is an optimal choice. Referrals can be obtained for your geographic area from Postpartum Support International: www.psidirectory.net, or call or text: 1-800-944-4773. You can also check with your insurance or employee assistance plan for providers.

- **Support groups**: therapy or peer support offered in a group setting to provide a space to learn about, normalize and gain tools for your postpartum mental health. Check with your birth center or hospital, or search for "postpartum therapy groups" in your local area. Postpartum Support International offers free online groups. See: www.postpartum.net/psi-online-support-meetings/.

- **Medication**: Medication can be an important part of improving symptoms for many moms with PMAD. It's a choice to consider thoughtfully with a trusted medical provider. Typically, a psychiatrist, OBGYN, or medical doctor will prescribe medication. Choose a doctor who is well-versed in pregnancy and lactation, if you are breastfeeding and can answer your questions about whether medication is right for you. Mother To Baby is an organization with excellent information about medications in pregnancy and lactation: www.mothertobaby.org.

- **Intensive treatment**: If these options are not feeling like enough to manage symptoms, concentrated treatment options are available such as intensive outpatient programs (IOP), offering support for most of the day, several days, and returning home at night. Staying in a treatment center or hospital overnight for several nights is another option, until you feel better and can maintain a regular routine to take care of yourself. Some centers allow your baby to come with you. Contact your doctor, therapist, psychiatrist, or insurance for referrals.

- **Additional supports that can boost mental wellness:**
  - Get stretches of consolidated sleep (see chapter six for more information)

- Go outside and get moderate exposure to sunlight daily
- Increase your support (see chapter four for more)
- Eat nutritious food
- Exercise regularly (once cleared by your doctor and in ways gentle to your body)
- Journal or use a perinatal mental health workbook
- Increase your social contact (call friends, try a mom's group, accept uplifting visitors)

"What we need are people to surround mama and care for her and the home and the other children and prepare meals and clean and listen. We need people surrounding mama that are aware of the signs and symptoms of postpartum mood or other health warning signs so someone else, who isn't tired and wounded and healing and overwhelmed and scared, can say, 'Hey, I'm going to call the doctor.'"

—JESSICA

TANIA'S STORY

Tania was born and raised in Mexico, got her university degrees in the US, and later moved to Germany. We met in grad school as we became therapists. She is a warm, authentic, funny, and driven woman with playful eyes, amazing eyebrows, and dark hair.

Tania underwent extensive fertility treatments to conceive her first child. When he was a year old, she found out she had become spontaneously pregnant again. "The surprise of being able to be pregnant again, naturally, felt unimaginable, beautiful, but very, very daunting. And yes, it was too soon," she said. "I was riddled with anxiety the whole pregnancy. When he was born, I remember I was not feeling well. I was crying a lot, and I couldn't function very well. I started wondering, 'What's happening with me?'" She made the connection she may have postpartum anxiety and depression.

She consulted her OBGYN and saw a therapist. Neither understood postpartum mental health and quickly invalidated her experience. This was painful, but she continued to advocate for herself. She found a maternal mental health unit at a hospital. She was connected with a psychiatrist who validated her symptoms but suggested attending a treatment program, as is customary in Germany as a first line of treatment before medication. This wasn't feasible for Tania. Finally, she was prescribed medication. She started to feel better.

When pregnant with her third child, "It was very much part of my care throughout my pregnancy and postpartum to make sure I didn't experience postpartum anxiety and depression again. I have therapy. I have a psychiatrist. I'm very vocal about how I feel. And I reach out," she said. "A trigger for me is lack of sleep, so I rest as much as I can." Tania worked out a schedule so she can get an additional hour or more of sleep once she gets her older kids off to school in the morning, while her husband or nanny watches the baby. "That makes a huge difference."

Her advice for other moms is, "Get informed, empower yourself, and advocate for yourself. I know it's hard, but make sure you have a support system, however that needs to look for you. As moms, especially new moms, we tend to put our needs to the side." But we still need to be a priority.

EXERCISES FOR REFRAMING

KEEP TABS ON YOUR MENTAL HEALTH

You have a lot to track when you are pregnant or have a new baby. Keeping tabs on how you are doing mentally may not register high on your list but is still important. Mental health is the foundation we operate from for all other aspects of life. How can you monitor your mental health in an accessible way? If you are already concerned you currently have a PMAD, skip to the next exercise.

WAYS TO WORK IT IN

Discuss your mental health together with your partner and agree on a way to address any concerns about each other. Designate a trusted person in your life to keep an eye on you and decide a plan of action if they notice symptoms (give them your resources from the next exercise). Use a mood-tracking app to record information about how you are feeling and check for any trends. Alert your therapist you are concerned about your perinatal mental health and ask for their help in tracking with you. Request a mental health screening from your doctor if they do not offer one.

Decide on the way that feels best for you to monitor your mental health and write your plan here.

KNOW YOUR RESOURCES

What resources are available to you if you need them for mental health? What modalities of treatment seem most feasible for you? If you are concerned about your mental health now, what is your plan of action to get help?

WAYS TO WORK IT IN

Ask your doula, midwife, OBGYN, hospital, birth center, birth educator, or other perinatal provider for recommendations for mental health support. Search online for resources in your area such as support groups. Reach out to Postpartum Support International to find a therapist, support group, or psychiatrist. Ask a trusted friend, family member, or partner to help you find resources. Understand your benefits through your insurance, such as therapy sessions. Call or text the National Maternal Health Hotline for non-emergency support twenty-four seven at 1-833-TLC-MAMA (1-833-852-6262).

Identify the resources that would be helpful for recovery from any anticipated or current mental health challenges such as a perinatal mental health therapist, support group, etc.

If you need help now, what is the easiest step you can take to start the process of getting support? How can you build from there?

TAKEAWAYS

1. Pregnancy and postpartum is a vulnerable time for mental health due to the significant life changes, hormonal factors, and lack of sleep. One in five women will experience a mental health disorder in pregnancy or the year following birth.

2. Beyond just postpartum depression, we now understand mental health can include a variety of experiences, called perinatal mood and anxiety disorders (PMAD). Dads, adoptive parents, and non-birthing parents can also experience mental health disorders.

3. PMAD are treatable, and options include individual therapy, support groups, and medication. Other steps can help, such as increasing support, getting consolidated sleep, and going outside daily.

If you find yourself checking off some of the symptoms listed in the chapter, it's not your fault, and you're not alone. You deserve help and can be well again. Start somewhere, even if it is just telling a friend or partner. This can break down the barrier of stigma and allow you to take another step forward. Regardless of how much you identified with information in this chapter, thank you for reading it. You never know when this knowledge might benefit you or another mom you know. It could save a life.

The next chapter discusses the shame around having "bad" thoughts about motherhood and the truth about how normal negative thoughts actually are.

MOTHERHOOD MYTH #9:
GOOD MOMS DON'T HAVE BAD THOUGHTS

"Why are all the other mothers able to quiet their babies and I can't? What's wrong with me?"

This is what I thought while driving home from baby-and-me yoga. The class was held in a beautiful, sunny studio with flowing white curtains and glossy wood floors. Our instructor led us through an hour of gentle movement together with our babies, winding down into baby massage. At the end of class, the instructor brought the volume down to a whisper as all the babies were relaxed and sleepy, and the mothers enjoyed a meditation. That was my cue to step outside to shush and soothe my son, the only baby who was crying. After class, I hurriedly packed up my diaper bag and yoga mat and held in my tears until I got to the car with my screaming baby. The other moms gave me sympathetic looks, but it felt like they were judging me just as harshly as I was judging myself.

I tried a couple more yoga classes with the same result and gave up. I pivoted to baby-and-me barre class instead. It was a little more upbeat—maybe my baby didn't like the "oms."

This time it was the loud music that bothered him. More crying. More frustration. Then the thoughts would bubble up:

I'm not good at being a mom.

My son deserves a better mom.

I can't do this. I don't want to do this anymore. I hate this. I want my old life back.

That's terrible! What are you thinking? A good mom doesn't have bad thoughts like that.

Did you see that reprimand come in at the end? Not only did I have bad thoughts about myself, but I layered on guilt and shame about those thoughts on top of it. This is especially toxic, I later found out.

Research shows most moms have "bad" or negative thoughts about motherhood at times. A 2021 study found 63 percent of new mothers also thought they were a "bad mother" some of the time. But the mothers who additionally feel guilt and shame are more likely to experience depression (Law, Hall, and Cheshire 2021, 1831–1845).

If we enter motherhood attached to the idea it will all be bliss and beauty, our expectation is we will love it all. But this creates tension with the lived experience of matrescence. Like the rest of life, you will experience both lovely and rough moments.

In motherhood, you may feel tired and broken. When baby vomit is on you all day because you couldn't fit a shower in, you may wonder, "How have I become a person that allows themselves to smell like vomit all day?" When you would like to do something for yourself, and you can't because the needs of your child must come first… When you wish you could reverse time and not have a baby, even for a few minutes…

And with these moments, you will naturally have the thoughts to match—"bad" thoughts about motherhood or your child. That's perfectly okay, because unless you act on them, thoughts are just thoughts. They are a manifestation of your brain processing information and experiences. Allow yourself permission to think and feel whatever comes up for you. It's all fair game. Nothing is bad or shameful about you for not loving every minute, and no need to add self-judgment to your to-do list.

I have such tenderness now for the version of myself who had those defeated thoughts and feelings. I was too exhausted and inexperienced to know my baby's behavior had little to do with me. I was not in control of him. Over time, I realized my baby had his own unique temperament, and sometimes he would cry without any reason at all. This was a developmental phase he went through, and no amount of planning, feeding, clean diapers, comforting, or clothing adjustments would have changed how he behaved. I was giving my best effort, and the crying wasn't a reflection of my worth as a mother. With time, education, and the experience of working with other moms, I discovered acknowledgment and compassion are some of the most powerful tools to use in the tough moments of motherhood.

Matrescence brings a wide range of thoughts and feelings. If you judge, criticize, ignore, or deny parts of your experience, it creates more negative feelings to deal with, like guilt and shame. Even the hard parts contribute to the whole of matrescence, and there are many strategies available to cope.

JASMINE'S STORY

Jasmine was the mother of a young, energetic girl. When she became my client, she had just left an abusive relationship with her daughter's dad. She worked hard to take care of her daughter, find her footing as a single mom, and pursue a career that would support them independently. This was difficult, draining work, and sometimes she felt exasperated by her spirited child.

In a therapy session with me one day, she confessed, "Sometimes I don't like my daughter. I love her, but sometimes I don't like her. Is that okay?" Her eyes welled up, and we held that statement tenderly. *Yes.* Sometimes we love people and don't like them. Sometimes we have feelings toward our children that feel taboo. All of it is a valid part of our experience.

I was proud of Jasmine for being able to say these words out loud, and it seemed like a pressure had been released. When she shared these thoughts with me and I reflected compassion back to her, it gave her permission to embrace the full experience of motherhood without the need to add shame and guilt to already difficult feelings. Because she shared this, we discovered what she needed: to self-soothe in those moments, to have breaks, to reconnect with the things that made her feel like her own person outside of motherhood, and to know she could have these thoughts and still be a good mother.

REAL THOUGHTS FROM REAL MOMS

To normalize how most moms have negative thoughts from time to time, here are samples of negative thoughts from real moms. If a negative thought crosses your mind, you are not alone and you are not a bad mother. A thought is just a thought.

"This was a mistake. I've ruined three people's lives. Why did I decide to go through with this? I was not trained for this. How would anyone think that I should be in charge of a child? Please, please, please stop crying! I can't think when you're crying!"

—ALICE A.

"To just leave. Leave my whole family."

—ANONYMOUS, NEW YORK CITY, NEW YORK

"Better moms are out there who seem to do it effortlessly."

—ANONYMOUS, SAN DIEGO, CALIFORNIA

"My kid would not a be a good human because of the things I
lived through or could not do right. For example, deploying
or working a ton due to the demands of my job, not being
there for pick up, and her having to be in daycare."

—KELLY B.

"I'm ruining my kids."

—ANONYMOUS, ARIZONA

"When I had a child with colic, who cried constantly for the
first three months, I just kept wishing things were different."

—ANONYMOUS, CALIFORNIA

"'This isn't how I thought it would be' as I was sleep deprived,
holding a crying infant and my four-year-old son suggested
that the baby and I should go back to the hospital because
he was irritated by the crying."

—DANIELLE

"I was going to drop my son. I was not going to feed him
enough or know what he needed. I'm not enough for him."

—TANYA G.

"One night when my first born was a few months old and
would not stop crying I told her I wish I'd never had her,
that she was making me miserable."

—ANONYMOUS, CALIFORNIA

"What is this shit? Why is this shit so hard? I don't have patience for this shit. I'm losing my shit. What have I done (specifically after having my second kid)? I also have recurring feelings of disappointment that society has created motherhood as we know it currently, envious of those who aren't moms, and anger when the deck feels stacked against me."

—ALYSSA S.

"I was angry at my body and what it couldn't do. I was angry that I wasn't always the mother I wanted to be. I was mad at those before me (friends and family) who I felt lied about the realities of motherhood."

—JESSICA

COPING WITH TOUGH MOMENTS AND NEGATIVE THOUGHTS

Every mother has difficult moments, and negative thoughts often follow. Many tools are within reach to cope in these times. Here are some strategies:

SELF-COMPASSION

An excellent antidote to judging and criticizing your experiences, self-compassion starts by treating yourself with the same kindness and compassion you might offer others. "Instead of just ignoring your pain with a 'stiff upper lip' mentality, you stop to tell yourself, 'This is really difficult right now. How can I comfort and care for myself in this moment?'" says Kristin Neff, a pioneer in the field of self-compassion (2023).

Self-compassionate people are gentle with themselves in the face of suffering, failure, or feeling inadequate. They acknowledge some degree of pain, imperfection, and vulnerability is a part of life. They can also put their situation into a larger perspective and recognize feelings without getting too reactive to them (Neff 2023).

Ways to practice self-compassion include:
- Noticing when you are critical of yourself and softening your self-talk to be more comforting and supportive.
- Using soothing touch for yourself like stroking your arms gently, placing your hand over your heart, or giving yourself a light squeeze like a hug.
- Talking to yourself how you would talk to a dear friend going through a difficult time, or how a caring friend would talk to you.
- Asking, "What does my heart need to hear right now?" and giving a kind answer.
- Acknowledging when things are hard—for example, "This is stressful," "This hurts," or "This is really difficult for me right now."
- Reminding yourself you are not suffering alone: "Other moms are going through this too," or "Everybody struggles."

I have additional exercises at the end of the chapter to help you put self-compassion into practice. Kristin Neff's website is also an excellent resource for learning more: Self-compassion.org.

MINDFULNESS

Mindfulness is turning your focus toward and noticing the present moment without judgment. It's an alternative to ruminating about the past, worrying about the future, or reprimanding yourself in the present. Studies indicate mindfulness helps with stress, sleep, pain, depression, anxiety, and more (Zhang 2021, 41–57). You can practice anywhere, at any time. Here is how:

- **Engage your senses**: Land in this moment. What is it like to be in your body right now—the sensation where your seat meets your chair or your hands hold this book? How does the temperature feel to you? Listen: Are there noises in your background? The refrigerator humming or a plane flying by? Breathe deep. Are there any scents? Look around you and notice your environment—the lighting, the wall color, the plants, the rug.
- **Breathe deeply**: Make breathing your sole focus by counting four seconds to inhale, taking a slight pause, then counting four seconds to exhale. Extend to five seconds to inhale and exhale, then six, and so on until you've reached a pace that fully fills your lungs. How does this expansion compare to your normal breathing?
- **Observe your baby**: Hold your baby, and take them in. What color are their eyes? Are they looking back at you? Be right there with them, and return their gaze. What does the weight of their body or the softness of their skin feel like in your arms? Take in the smell of their little head. Hear their sounds of breathing, sucking, or cooing. Bring awareness to this moment with your baby in all the ways available to you.

- **Scan your body**: Slow your breath, and tune into your body. Start at your head and work your way down. Notice if you have any tension in your forehead and release it. Check for tightness in your mouth or jaw and let it go. Release your neck, and let your shoulders fall away from your ears. Shake out your arms and let them hang. Continue this progression down to your toes, surrendering any tenseness as you go. Scan your body once more to let go of any remaining tension.
- **Put on baby goggles**: Babies are masters of mindfulness. They take things in with wonder. They don't judge or get caught up in their thoughts. Imagine the world through their fresh eyes: how they delight in the bathwater or marvel at the pigeons on a walk in the park. Notice right alongside them and be in their moment too.

How does it feel when you practice mindfulness? Do you notice any shifts in your mind, mood, or body? Many apps and websites offer more ideas for mindfulness practices and guided meditations. Try practicing in everyday moments to help you access mindfulness more easily when you need it in stressful times.

NAMING YOUR FEELINGS AND NEEDS

When you name your feelings, you are validating your internal experience. It helps you make sense of your thoughts.

Why are my thoughts spiraling out of control?

Ah—it's because I'm feeling exhausted and demoralized.

This process provides important information about what you need and how to address those needs. When you name the problem, you can decide on the solution. In difficult moments, it is a relief to remember you still have agency and choices.

Here is a sequence to make these connections between feelings, needs, and options. As an example, consider my story at the beginning of the chapter:

1. **Notice your thoughts**: "Why are all the other mothers able to quiet their babies and I can't? What's wrong with me?"
2. **Name your feelings**: Inadequate, frustrated, exasperated.
3. **Identify your needs**: I need some assurance that I am doing a good enough job as a parent and to know I'm not alone in having trouble soothing my baby.
4. **Brainstorm your options**: I could call my mother-in-law and ask her if she had trouble soothing her babies or grandbabies. I could reach out to my pediatrician, a postpartum doula, or a parent educator to help me assess my situation. Maybe I'll tell my husband about this and get his help to address the situation together.

Through this process, choices become available, instead of just a swirling mashup of emotions and harsh thoughts. You can choose which action you feel most drawn to and try it.

Identifying emotions is not second nature to everyone. It may take practice to get attuned to your feelings and name them.

For example, as you're changing your baby's diaper in the morning, you could check in:

What am I feeling?

What do I need?

Sometimes looking at options helps us identify our emotions. Below is a list to get you started. Emotion card decks, mood tracking apps, and emotion emoji charts are available if you need more options.

Amused	Embarrassed
Angry	Empathy
Anxious	Envious
Avoidant	Excited
Bittersweet	Expectant
Bored	Exhausted
Belonging	Fearful
Calm	Frustrated
Compassion	Grief
Confusion	Guilty
Connection	Happy
Contempt	Hateful
Content	Heartbroken
Curious	Hopeless
Defensive	Humiliated
Dehumanized	Humility
Despair	Hurt
Discouraged	Insecure
Disappointed	Interested
Disgusted	Invisible

Jealous
Joyful
Lonely
Love
Nostalgic
Overwhelmed
Pride
Regretful
Relieved
Resigned
Resentful

Sad
Self-righteous
Shameful
Stressed
Surprised
Tranquil
Trusting
Worried
Vulnerable

TAKING A SAFE BREAK

At times, thoughts and feelings are so intense you need a break from your baby in order to calm down.

If someone else is available, ask them to take the baby while you have a breather. If you are alone, set the baby down in a safe place such as their crib, bassinet, or swing, and step away for a few minutes. You want your baby to know you are consistently available to meet their needs, but it will not harm your child for you to take an occasional, brief break. In fact, this could be safest for both of you. Try one of the strategies for self-soothing during your break.

SELF-CARE

Self-care can answer some of the longings behind negative thoughts and emotions and builds resilience against harsh thoughts in the first place. It affirms your needs still matter. What are authentic and accessible ways to bring self-care into motherhood? Let's start with a clear definition.

Self-care: doing what you need to sustain yourself and re-balance depletion. It is also *claiming time* to do those things, *acknowledging your own worth*, and *creating and upholding boundaries* to honor yourself.

Caring for yourself may take on a new and basic form in new motherhood. It could be taking a shower, making sure to eat regularly, brushing your teeth, applying deodorant, or taking a walk. There are no rules to self-care other than matching your actions to what restores you in a manageable way. Bethany Warren, a licensed clinical social worker, postpartum workbook author, and certified perinatal mental health provider shared, "Sometimes it is picking one small thing to weave back into everyday life. Once that is a more regular practice, then we can reevaluate and think about what else do you need now? What are you missing?"

A common barrier Warren sees for mothers is guilt. "Guilt is such a liar," she said. "Oftentimes it shows up in ways that are so distorted and illogical." She notices how it acts as a stop sign for her clients, telling them they are doing something bad. "You're taking five minutes to yourself and you feel guilty. Your partner has your baby so you can finally get some respite—you feel guilty. You're gonna go move your body—you feel guilty."

She works with her clients to recognize how and where guilt tends to show up, and to move forward anyway. One strategy is having an internal dialogue with guilt, "Oh, there you are, again. You're not gonna stop me, but I see you," or "Come on, Guilt. We're going on our walk anyway."

"Self-care is not just the fufu stuff, even though those things are important too, if you're able to do them. It's sometimes things like setting boundaries with who can come visit the baby or being protective of your energy," said Warren.

Try an experiment: If you lean into taking care of yourself, how does it influence your thoughts and feelings? Does it help you show up as the mom you want to be? See the exercises at the end of the chapter for how to develop a self-care practice.

WHEN ARE "BAD" THOUGHTS DANGEROUS?

Most "bad" thoughts are normal and harmless, but some indicate you need support. Get immediate help if you experience any of the following:

- Thoughts become disruptive to your life or functioning (example: you're having trouble taking care of yourself or your baby because you are so weighed down by thinking you are an unfit mom).
- Thoughts become difficult to control or distressing (example: repeated thoughts of dropping your baby keep popping into your mind and you can't get them to stop).
- Feeling like you may *act* on dangerous thoughts, such as harming your baby, harming yourself or someone else, or abandoning your baby. *This is a mental health emergency. Call or text the national crisis hotline at 9-8-8, or call 9-1-1.*

For non-emergency support, call or text the National Maternal Mental Health Hotline to speak with someone twenty-four seven at 1-833-TLC-MAMA (1-833-852-6262). For support and connection with resources in your local area, call or text the Postpartum Support International Helpline (leave a message and get a response during business hours): 1-800-944-4773. You can also reach out to your physician, a therapist, or psychiatrist for help with troublesome thoughts.

For more information on mental health, see chapter eight and the resources section at the back of the book.

. . . .

EXERCISES FOR REFRAMING

. . . .

PRACTICE SELF-COMPASSION

This exercise gives you a way to try out self-compassion with a low-stakes situation, so it's available when you need it in other contexts.

WAYS TO WORK IT IN

Create a window of five to ten minutes to try this during a lunch break or baby's nap. You can also check out the self-compassion audio exercises at Self-compassion.org. Narrate your self-compassion to your baby.

Imagine a situation that was slightly distressing for you (think a three on a scale of one to ten, where ten is highly distressing). For example, gum got stuck on your shoe, you forgot your transit pass and have to wait to buy a ticket for the subway, or you don't have an umbrella and it starts raining. What happened? How did it feel in your body? What thoughts did you have?

Practice self-compassion by imagining you could go back and talk to yourself in that moment. Acknowledge and comfort yourself. Here is some sample language:

"This is really frustrating for me. I'm facing a very human challenge."

"That's so awful you got gum on your shoe! This has happened to a lot of other people too. You'll get through this."

"We all forget our transit pass sometimes. Take some deep breaths and forgive yourself."

Write the language here that feels right to you.

Is there any physical soothing you'd like right now, such as stroking your arms or a hand on your heart?

What shifts did you notice when trying this? What is the most effective part for you?

The next time you are hard on yourself or facing a challenge, see if you can try self-compassion. When you practice regularly, it will become more automatic.

DEFINE YOUR SELF-CARE

Use this exercise to kick start self-care as a regular practice. When you have ideas ready to work from, it will be easier to get started in a time of need.

WAYS TO WORK IT IN

Find fifteen to thirty minutes to consider these questions. Jot them down before bed, think them over while feeding your baby, or request a support person watch your baby while you do this. Talk the questions over with your partner and discover each other's picture of self-care.

What are the reasons taking care of yourself is important? Why are you worth it?

Think of a time in the past when you felt balanced and nourished. What was it like? What helped you feel that way? If you can't think of a past time, what's your guess about what is nourishing and rebalancing for you?

What does this tell you about what self-care looks like for you? List ideas for self-care here:

What are manageable ways to bring these ideas into motherhood?

What might the barriers be to practice self-care in motherhood, and how can you overcome them?

What support or boundaries do you need to make self-care happen?

TAKEAWAYS

1. Most women have "bad" thoughts sometimes about motherhood or their babies. This is a normal experience. When we add guilt and shame, it makes us feel worse and even fuels depression.
2. Give yourself permission to think and feel what comes. When you accept all thoughts and feelings as part of your

experience, you are validating and staying connected to yourself through the process of matrescence.

3. Self-compassion, mindfulness, identifying feelings and needs, safe breaks, and self-care are tools available to navigate the tough moments of motherhood.

I wish I could go back and share many things with my new-mother self, especially the tools from this chapter. I hope you find one or more of them that feels nourishing to you, and it helps sustain you through new motherhood and beyond.

The next chapter delves into relationships after baby. As with many other parts of our lives in new motherhood, our relationships experience shifts too. Don't worry! I'll share the concrete things you can do to strengthen your relationship in new parenthood.

A BABY BRINGS YOU CLOSER

Ah, becoming a family.

I wanted the experience to feel like a birth announcement photo. My husband and I gazing lovingly into each other's eyes, cradling the baby equally in our arms, and leaning over to kiss the sweet baby's head. So bonding, so peaceful, and so egalitarian.

A baby would snuggle into our existing partnership and strengthen our closeness. It would be like before the baby, but better! Because now we would be working as a team to support another life and sharing in new special moments together, all with balanced roles.

But this isn't always the trajectory for couples after having a baby. When I taught relationship classes for a new mother's group, I could see the real picture unfolding.

In class, the moms had their babies along in carriers, on blankets, and in arms, ranging in ages from a few weeks to a few months. We sat in a circle on the floor of an exercise studio, and the babies made all sorts of adorable and disruptive noises while the adults learned and discussed.

I told the group there is a spectrum of normal emotions and experiences for couples after having a baby. It ranges from a new sense of closeness to intense feelings of disconnection and resentment.

Most couples (67 percent) experience a decrease in relationship satisfaction after having their first baby (Gottman and Schwartz Gottman 2007, 5). I asked the group their opinion on why couples feel less satisfied. The answers came pouring out:

"We don't have time for each other anymore. It's all focused on the baby."

"We're just so tired."

"We have a lot more to manage."

"We're fighting more. We have a lot of decisions now, and we're more on edge."

"My partner has no idea what I'm going through."

"He just walks out the door and goes surfing, and I'm stuck with the baby because I'm breastfeeding. It feels unfair."

"I'm not interested in sex."

"I feel jealous that my husband gets to go to work."

"I'm just surviving. I don't have the energy to focus on the relationship."

Inevitably, the moms asked me the burning question: "When will things go back to normal?"

My answer: They don't.

We don't have a timetable where a relationship snaps back to its pre-baby form, much like we don't have a timetable for our bodies to go back to how they used to be—and they may not. The truth is, having a baby creates a "new normal" in our relationships, one that accommodates the new central focus of loving and caring for a baby. It is possible to cultivate closeness, growth, and purpose together in this phase. But if a partnership gets off track after having a baby, it is up to the couple to take an active role in correcting their path. Without attention, the problems may linger.

The real picture for a couple with a new baby probably looks more like two exhausted humans who are proud, bewildered, cranky, a little duped, and more tired than they ever knew they could feel, holding a baby (who is cute as ever).

What the women in the new mother's group were seeking was hope—something they could reach for when their relationship was getting rocked by new parenthood. And we have hope: all is not all lost if your partnership is strained by the challenge of a baby. In fact, it's a great time to take stock and reassess what you need as a couple to cope with the ebb and flow of challenges that come your way in parenthood and in life. Many tools are available for healing and strengthening your relationship.

THE REFRAME: HAVING A BABY CREATES A "NEW NORMAL" IN YOUR RELATIONSHIP

Just as matrescence is a transformation for you as a woman, having a baby creates transformation in your relationship, a "new normal." You and your partner can take tangible steps to stay or get back on track with your relationship.

HOW BABIES TRANSFORM RELATIONSHIPS

Countless clients came through my office for couples' therapy telling a version of the same narrative: "Things changed after we had kids." I heard this from new parents to couples who already launched their children to college. This makes sense, because the transformation of becoming parents and caring for a baby can be a huge shift in a relationship. Time together is less available. New conflicts can arise around parenting and role responsibility. There may be less time, energy, and interest in intimacy. Meanwhile, everyone is exhausted and more on edge, and communication breaks down.

I checked with Kimberly Panganiban, a mom and marriage and family therapist certified in the Gottman Method of couples' therapy, about what she sees in her private practice when couples become parents.

"What people struggle with the most is negotiating their new roles and responsibilities and finding time for the relationship," Panganiban says. Couples who previously had a division of labor at home grapple with the influx of new tasks around caring for a baby and are often shocked by the responsibility parenthood requires.

She frequently sees a split of household labor along gender lines for heterosexual couples, with most of the childcare falling on women. "There starts to be a division between them that causes a lot more conflict… They have to take the time to talk about those things and figure it out. And some couples do, and some couples don't."

As for finding time together, she says, "There's just hardly time to shower and pee. So, for many new parents, even the thought of finding a sitter, getting dressed up, paying money to go out to dinner—everything that used to be fun—just feels like a chore and kind of overwhelming. They don't know how to find new ways to connect or spend time together, and the ways that they used to are less viable or just not easy." This can lead to a feeling of distance and a sense of, "What happened to us? Is it ever going back to normal?" "I think they're surprised by the impact it actually has on the relationship. They know they're not going to be able to spend as much time together, but not how important that is to their relationship and to their connection."

To get back on track, Panganiban recommends starting to talk about it. "Even saying, 'We're not spending time together and it sucks. We're feeling disconnected.' Having that conversation makes it feel better, just both knowing they're feeling the same, and it's not the way they want it to be. Putting that out in the open is helpful," she said. "Ideally, they would also figure out creative ways to stay connected to one another."

She suggests considering what fosters connection. "Is it through touch, or spending time together, or showing appreciation? Understanding what each person needs in order to feel connection and how they could integrate that into their lives even in small ways."

Another tip is to discuss roles and responsibilities. "Who does what, how would they like that to work, and how does that relate to their history? Understanding and unpacking all of that, so they can then figure out a division of labor that feels fair to both of them." This will be discussed more in the next section.

Panganiban encourages, "Don't lose sight that your relationship needs care and attention just like your baby does. Things are going to be different, and they're going to be hard, but it doesn't last forever." The phase when a child needs you so acutely as a baby will pass.

STRENGTHENING YOUR RELATIONSHIP

How can couples steer their relationships back on track or keep them there in the first place? Below is a roundup of relationship-enhancing behaviors that are good for all new parents, and especially if parenthood has made things more challenging. You don't have to try them all at once. Choose one that speaks to you and build from there.

Read this with your partner. This information is not for you alone, and the responsibility does not rest solely on you to keep your relationship afloat. Use this as a tool to get on the same page and work together toward your mutual happiness.

CHECK IN

Becoming parents is a significant time of transition for both of you. Check in with each other and ask how it's going—then listen. You don't have to fix it. The most value will be in demonstrating you heard each other. For couples going through life changes, I recommend a weekly check in so time is carved out to make it happen, even just ten minutes.

EXPRESS NEEDS

A common pitfall for couples with a baby is scorekeeping. Because they have much more to do, and all independent activities require coordinating childcare, what each person does comes under the microscope. When one person strolls out the door to the gym and their partner is at home with the fussy baby, it's hard not to make a mental tally mark on the scoreboard of things *they* got to do, but *I* didn't. The catch: score keeping builds resentment, and no one wins because it's difficult to keep things completely even. Does going to work count as unencumbered alone time? Is making dinner an even trade for doing the dishes? It's tough to sort it all out.

Expressing what you each need is an alternative that can diffuse score-keeping mentality. If you're resentful your partner got to go to the gym, you can say, "I want to get a workout in. Can you watch the baby for an hour?" Communicating directly ensures your needs are known and affirms you still matter in a time when you are giving so much to your baby. Sometimes we wait for our partner to notice what we want or expect they should "get it." This does not increase the chances your needs will be met and keeps you waiting. Even the most amazing of partners cannot read minds.

Make needs expression easier with supports such as a shared calendar or posted schedule where time is blocked out automatically—things like time with friends, dates together, or opportunities to exercise. Agree that it is taboo to schedule over these time blocks without permission. See the exercises at the end of the chapter for support.

DISTRIBUTE RESPONSIBILITIES

Who does the dishes? Who scoops the litter box? The addition of new responsibilities of baby care calls for a shift in task management to make things more balanced. Have a discussion together of who does what by taking an inventory of recurring tasks and dividing the workload. This can go a long way toward feeling you and your partner are working as a team, fending off resentment, and reducing guilt for leisure time.

In addition, agree on a strategy to manage things that come up spontaneously. This could be a shared note or task-tracking app, a list on paper, or a weekly discussion to capture things like "fill out paperwork for day care" or "investigate the weird smell in the laundry room." This way, both partners have an opportunity to see what miscellaneous tasks have to be completed and decreases the chance of one person carrying the invisible mental burden of a running list.

Eve Rodsky, author of the book *Fair Play*, suggests when one person takes on a task, they are responsible for the entire process—start to finish—including conceiving, planning, and executing (Rodsky 2019, 114–115). For example, "taking the dog to the vet" means scheduling the appointment, showing up with the dog, paying the bill, and coordinating any follow up.

Decide on a point to reevaluate responsibilities and speak up if the balance gets out of whack. Suffering silently with an unbalanced workload does not ultimately serve your relationship.

This process doesn't have to be dull. You can conduct a "fantasy task draft" and take turns choosing your tasks or make a card deck of responsibilities and deal them out. *Fair Play* offers a "game" to distribute tasks.

NEGOTIATE ROLES

Think of yourselves a parenting team. What will your individual roles be in raising a child? Will one parent stay home and the other work? Will you both work and manage the household together? In what ways do you each want to be involved with your child? Sometimes couples can slide into roles that feel unsatisfying. They don't have to stay that way. Discuss roles to see if you can achieve balance for your family. A structure for talking about roles can be found in the exercises at the end of the chapter.

SHARE APPRECIATION

Appreciation is an instant love-boost and one of the first homework assignments I give my clients in couples' therapy. When we express appreciation, it makes the other person feel acknowledged and has the added benefit of telling them what we like so we might get more of it. The research of John Gottman found expressing appreciation is a behavior that leads to more satisfying relationships (Gottman and Schwartz Gottman 2007, 149–150).

Try telling each other something you appreciate daily through a conversation, a text, or a note. Make this a mutual exercise, so it doesn't feel one-sided. It could be, "I really appreciated when you noticed I needed a break and offered to hold the baby today. It helped me reset," or "Thank you for cleaning up after that diaper blow-out." Giving specific examples makes the appreciations juicier, but all appreciations are good. What do you notice when you appreciate each other?

SPEND TIME AS A COUPLE

It may be hard to come by once baby arrives, but couple time is still possible and helps relationships feel more connected. A regular date is a great way to hold space for your relationship. It doesn't have to be lavish. A "date" can be anywhere, anytime, doing anything—so long as it is time together and mutually enjoyable. It could be having a conversation or watching a show together in your living room, or taking a drive while your baby naps in the backseat. Avoid talking only about logistics during your date. Carve out this time to be pleasurable.

Someday, your child will be older, and it will be easier to get a sitter for a night out or meet for lunch while your child is at school. Until then, brainstorm together what is possible to keep connection alive, and commit to a time to make it happen on a regular basis that is manageable for you.

SPEND TIME AS A FAMILY

I cherish the photos and memories of my husband holding our tiny newborns and changing their diapers. Watching him become a father was a process that brought me joy. Slowing down and taking time to witness the wonders of parenting and the growth you are both undergoing in the transition to parenthood can be a bonding experience worth making time for. You are forming another relationship in the process: a *family* relationship. This needs its own space to develop.

SPEND TIME APART

Having time to nurture your own needs and identity is critical to a healthy relationship. Panganiban says this allows individuals "to bring a better self to your partner and your relationship" and to decrease the likelihood of more miscommunication, conflict, and misunderstanding. Ensure you each have opportunities for time away from your baby to do something enjoyable for yourselves and get restored, even in small doses.

GET SUPPORT

Here's yet another reason to get support: It can benefit your relationship. When you have resources outside your partnership to help with the physical and emotional demands of parenting, it reduces the load on your relationship. Support can be for your whole family, not just for the baby or birth mom.

TALK ABOUT INTIMACY

Birthing mothers are frequently less interested in sex postpartum due to pelvic pain, hormonal vaginal dryness and low libido, fatigue, or feeling "touched out." Some couples may have already been in a sexual slump during pregnancy and wondering how to recover. All of this makes it an opportune time to talk openly about sex and discover together: Is sex possible now, or do we need to wait? What are the options for physical connection or intimacy that are available to us (think holding hands, kissing, snuggling, massage, oral sex, etc.)? How would we like to signal to each other we are interested in intimacy? What is a way to turn down sex that doesn't feel like a shutdown? More information can be found in the "Spotlight on Sex" in chapter five.

WHEN TO GET HELP

If you're having trouble navigating relationship challenges on your own, couples' therapy can help. Panganiban suggests therapy for couples who have more conflict, decreasing connection, unfair division of labor, or the relationship feels more negative than positive. Look for a provider who has advanced training in working with couples, and ask about their approach to assess if it is a good fit. Many therapists offer sessions online, making them easier to access for new parents. There may be clinics in your community that offer low-fee services if you are concerned about cost.

Couples' workshops are another option: group experiences for skill building, education, and connection that meet for a consolidated time, such as a weekend or weekly for six weeks. Even reading or listening to a book together can be helpful. Most couples wait too long to engage help and then have more to work through when they do. You don't need to delay until you are in crisis. Don't let stigma stop you from getting your relationship where you want it to be.

JANNA AND TROY'S STORY

Janna and Troy came to me for couples' therapy because they felt disconnected and unsure how to change course. A few years into having two children, they slid into a routine, and their relationship faded into the background. They worked, cared for the kids, and took care of home responsibilities. Troy had a variable work schedule, so there was often a different rhythm to their weeks and no dependable time they could spend together.

The missing connection was taking a toll on their relationship, especially for Janna. "I just want him to notice me and show me he's still interested in our relationship. I'm not sure if he is anymore," she said. Janna felt her efforts to connect were one-sided as she typically initiated arrangements for them to spend time together. She started wondering if Troy was having an affair. When I asked Troy about this, he was shocked. "I love Janna. I completely want to be with her. I just don't know what I need to do." They were stuck.

Progress for Janna and Troy required direct communication about their needs and awareness of where they came from. Sharing how the past played into their present-day needs built compassion and understanding between them. They also committed to spending time together and having regular dates. Troy made an effort to show interest in a meaningful way to Janna: physical touch. They signaled to each other when they wanted intimacy. They tried to make their everyday interactions count by paying attention and being present. With consistent efforts over time, they found their way back to each other. They were able to rebuild connection and sustain it through small daily acts that demonstrated how much they mattered to each other.

EXERCISES FOR REFRAMING

MAKE YOUR NEEDS KNOWN

If you weren't direct about your needs with your partner before having a baby, it's a great time to start. Make the expression of your needs direct, brief, and focused on what you do want (not what you don't). This way it is crystal clear.

To illustrate: "I need your help with the dishes at night," instead of "I need you to stop assuming I'll clean up after you all the time," or "I'd like you to watch the baby while I take a shower," instead of, "You never ask if I want a shower!"

Some examples of needs statements:

I need: twenty minutes alone, a walk around the neighborhood, time to visit my friends, to put real clothes on, to take a hot shower, or to talk about something other than the baby.

Sometimes I'll hear from new parents, "I don't even know what I need." A Needs Menu with more ideas can be found at the end of this chapter to help.

WAYS TO WORK IT IN

Review the Needs Menu, and express one need today. Make expressing your needs a daily or weekly practice. Review the needs list together with your partner and each choose a need you want fulfilled.

What need(s) would you like to express and get met? When will you make this request?

What system would you like to put in place to make it easier for needs to be regularly fulfilled (a shared calendar, schedule, etc.)?

DISCUSS ROLES EXPLICITLY

How do you see your role as a mother or father? Make this an explicit conversation with the questions below so you can see where you will settle in together and where compromise needs to take place.

WAYS TO WORK IT IN

Answer these questions together with your partner over dinner. Ponder the questions separately and come together for a discussion at an agreed upon time. Go somewhere inspiring with a great view to talk about it.

Ask: How do you envision your role as a parent? How would you like to be involved in raising our child?

Share: This is my ideal of our roles.

Where do we have common or shared ideas? Where do our ideas differ? Where can we be flexible to create a life we both enjoy?

What supports or resources do we each need to fulfill our shared ideal?

When will we reevaluate? Identify a time point and stick to it.

1. While social messages may highlight the sweetness and bonding of becoming a family, research indicates that most couples feel less satisfied with their relationships after having a baby.

2. Couples are often surprised by the stresses presented by parenthood: decreased focus on the relationship, less time together, negotiating new roles and responsibilities, more conflict, and less sex.

3. You can do tangible things to keep your partnership on track or course correct if your relationship is negatively impacted after having a baby, from discussing and dividing responsibilities to going to couples' therapy.

Keeping your relationship healthy takes repeated small efforts and behaviors over time. It can seem like a big undertaking, especially for tired and overwhelmed new parents, but putting in a little effort early can give you big rewards for your whole family. "The greatest gift you can give your baby is a happy and strong relationship between the two of you" (Gottman and Schwartz Gottman 2007, 27).

This chapter reframed the final motherhood myth. The next chapter will summarize core skills for matrescence as a reminder of tools you collected in this reading journey. Congratulations on all the work you have done so far to support yourself in matrescence.

NEEDS MENU

I need:

- You to watch the baby while I take a break
- You to do [household chore]
- A mother's helper, babysitter, postpartum doula, or nanny for consistent support
- A walk by myself/together
- For you to arrive home at [time] to give me a break
- Some quiet time alone
- Help with overnight feeding
- A nap
- More consolidated sleep
- Help getting the baby to sleep
- More time for my work/interests/self-care
- For you to take care of [task] regularly
- To outsource [tasks]
- To see a lactation consultant/therapist/psychiatrist/acupuncturist/chiropractor/coach/physical therapist/reiki healer/spiritual mentor/ nutritionist/etc.

- Help with sleep training
- You to learn more about baby care with me
- A hug/kiss when you leave
- You to ask me more questions/talk with me more
- To discuss our finances/have a savings plan
- You to be on my side
- To talk about non-baby things
- You to ask about [my aspirations, my work, my day, etc.] and really listen
- You to see that I am competent in taking care of the baby
- Your full attention when we talk
- To know you think I am sexy
- To feel more respected by you
- More appreciation or encouragement
- A weekly date night
- More intimacy/romance/sex
- To get dressed up and go out with you
- An adventure together
- An overnight without baby
- To cuddle, to be held
- More conversations where we are both getting our needs met
- To go to a couples workshop/therapy
- To see my friends/have a friend getaway
- To visit family
- Support in connecting with more friends
- A back rub/foot rub/massage
- A hot or cold drink
- More affection/physical touch
- To get my hair/nails done
- More time outdoors
- Time to exercise regularly

- A better balance between work and family
- More peace/calm/fun/creativity/spontaneity/structure in my life
- To discuss my return to work/that I don't want to return to work
- You to do half/more housework
- To feel less stressed/overwhelmed
- To do activities as a family
- To organize our time so we each get to do things for ourselves
- To reconnect with the _____ part of myself/my own interests
- To buy some new clothes
- Time to reflect on what would really restore me/help me feel like me
- To take a class I'm interested in
- To pursue a hobby
- To learn about my strengths
- To connect with my spirituality
- To go for a drive/hike/swim/climb
- To travel/plan a trip
- To research something I'm interested in
- To experience something new
- Nourishing meals
- To meditate/practice yoga/journal
- To watch a good show/movie/read a book
- An agreement that I will come to you when I am ready/interested in sex

CORE SKILLS FOR MATRESCENCE

Whether you read straight through from the beginning, or skipped around to get here, I invite you to bring it all together with this chapter. Summarized here are the skills from this book you can access at any time to stand grounded in the version of motherhood that best serves you. Think of these skills as ingredients for an elixir to keep you thriving in matrescence and stay liberated from the Motherhood Myths.

AWARENESS

Gather knowledge of what is reasonable to expect in motherhood based on data and real experiences.

ALIGNMENT

Stay true to the values, ideas, and behaviors that are most natural and congruent for you in motherhood.

LETTING GO

Release expectations about motherhood or yourself that feel excessive, unrealistic, out of alignment, or shame inducing, whether they were your ideas, someone else's, or a cultural or societal norm. Replace expectations with ideas that feel real and supportive.

EMBODIMENT

Be present in your experience of motherhood and welcome all the thoughts and feelings that come with it.

ADVOCACY

Develop a clear sense of what your needs are as you become a mother. Voice, ask, and find the match for your needs.

BOUNDARIES

Create limits around what and who you permit in your motherhood experience, how you protect your energy, and what is "enough."

INTUITION

Listen to what your truest inner voice tells you.

ACCEPTANCE

Acknowledge what is happening and understand it may not be in your control or your fault.

FLEXIBILITY

Adjust thinking, actions, and expectations in motherhood based on your lived experience and with the goal of having more ease.

SELF-COMPASSION

Give acknowledgement and empathy to yourself in the face of the hard moments and phases of motherhood.

APPRECIATION

Recognize what you, your body, and your partner are doing right.

CURIOSITY

Cultivate a mindset of interest in your experiences and outcomes as you learn, experiment, and grow.

GRACE

Give yourself space and forgiveness in the process of matrescence. Remember, it's like adolescence—with learning, awkward moments, and transformation into a new version of you.

SUPPORT

Access resources outside yourself to uplift, help, and heal you.

CONNECTION

Seek manageable ways to stay surrounded by others and keep important relationships alive. You're not alone in this.

CONCLUSION

Now you know the hidden side of the motherhood story: Women face significant challenges in the transition to parenthood and are under immense pressure to "do it all." Meanwhile, the infrastructure to sustain us is lacking. Moms carry a greater burden at home and in our heads. We are expected to be fully involved parents and, while we're at it, make ourselves and our lives look perfect. If we turn to motherhood myths as a guide, they fail us.

Coming away from this book, I hope you see becoming a mother as a transformation that requires space and grace, and that it may present both losses and new facets of your identity.

You may contend with noise about the right way to do things, changes in the structure of your life, and shifts in your relationships. Ultimately, *you* get to decide who you become through this transformation. Your own intuition and wisdom are your best guides. If you are struggling, support is available. Reach for it.

My hope in writing this book is to create a shift in how women prepare for parenthood. We do not need myths, silence, or misinformation. Support that is reactive to the hardships of becoming a mother is good, but it is not good enough.

Mothers deserve accurate information and robust preparation for the impact that becoming a parent will have for them as a person.

I believe this will not only create less personal suffering for mothers, but the positive impact will extend far beyond them, reaching their children, partners, communities, and workplaces. Mothers are an essential part of the fabric of our society, and the more we can help them to be healthy and well-adjusted, the better for us all. The deeper I wrote into this book, the more I believed in the power of real information for mothers.

A CLOSING RITUAL

My first therapist job was as a grief counselor at a hospice organization. Our training emphasized the value of rituals, particularly for transitions, partings, and closures. This honored the work and transformations that occurred and held space for the feelings around endings. Here is a parting ritual I offer you:

Imagine you are packing a bag for the journey into motherhood, just like you might for leaving to the hospital or birth center to have your baby, or for an outing with your infant. Only this bag is just for you, to carry what you need in your heart and mind as you become a mother.

What are the essentials you will need on this journey? Are there any old myths, ideas, or expectations that may add weight or take up space you no longer need to carry?

Consider what tools and insights you would like to take forward from this book. It may be the core skills from the previous chap-

ter, things you learned along the way, or "aha" moments from working the exercises. You decide what goes in and stays out. You can access your bag at any time in your journey for what you need. You can reorganize, clean it out, or repack it as you please.

Allow this book to remind you of what you intended to pack. It may be helpful to refer to from time to time as a touchstone. Your exercises will be here for you. The resources section is a good quick reference. Look to familiarize yourself with what's available to you.

I hope you also let this book be the foundation you can spring from if you need more to feel equipped for parenthood. You may have more questions, need more resources, or seek more facts. Ask trusted mothers. Engage with trustworthy professionals. Find what you need to launch into your best and most informed motherhood.

We can take charge of our preparation for motherhood and equip ourselves with sound knowledge. We can be ready for the challenges and know what to do when we face the hard parts. We can change the narrative with our own voices. We can raise our own families in congruence with our values. We can pave the way for fellow moms and expand our reach by being truthful and transparent about what motherhood is really like instead of holding up the myths.

THE BEST TRUTHS

Many of the stories I shared about my own transition to motherhood in this book highlight the struggles and hard parts because I wanted to be real about what to expect. I also want you to know motherhood is fascinating, growth-producing, and enriching. In closing, I'll share some of the best truths of my experience of motherhood with you:

- Creating bonds with my children that have exponentially expanded my concept of love
- Witnessing and sharing experiences through my children's lens that is full of wonder, play, and joy
- Laughing with and getting to know the amazing humans that my children are
- Having a role in life with an immense depth of meaning and purpose
- Seeing how I can rise to new challenges, develop new strengths, solve new problems, and create stronger boundaries
- Healing injuries to my child self through the actions I take as a parent
- Experiencing the grounding that comes from deep commitment and loyalty to my kids

May you experience all of this and more in your journey. May you feel ready for matrescence.

POSTPARTUM SUPPORT CHECKLIST

A place to capture all your postpartum support for easy reference.

☐ **My parenting values are:**

☐ **My strengths are:**

☐ **What I'm letting go of to define my version of enough:**

☐ **My words of self-compassion are:**

☐ **Supplies**: a list of supplies for my physical comfort post-partum (pads, pain relief spray, Ibuprofen, squirt bottle, nipple cream, etc.):

☐ **Meals**: my plan for easy, nutritious meals (meal train, meals made ahead and frozen, meal delivery, personal chef):

☐ **Coordinator**: someone who can help me organize re-sources, make announcements, hold boundaries (friend, partner, family member):

☐ **References**: my go-to resources if I have questions about baby (an experienced mom friend, pediatrician, trusted books):

□ **Visitors**: supportive and uplifting people who I would like to visit (helpful friends and family):

□ **Lactation support**: resources in my area, if planning to breastfeed, or for cessation support (lactation consultant, nurse hotline, breastfeeding group):

□ **Scheduled help**: someone to watch baby consistently while I shower, rest, or take a break (partner, family member, friend, or postpartum doula):

□ **Emergency help**: someone I could call if I need immediate help with the baby (partner, neighbor, friend, family member):

☐ **Physical healing**: my resources for supporting physical healing (my doctor's number or nurse line, acupuncture, physical therapy):

☐ **Sleep**: my plan for how to get consolidated stretches of sleep (alternate shifts with partner, get support for a day-time stretch, night nanny):

☐ **Monitoring mental health**: how I will keep tabs on my mental health (apps, designated person to check in, therapist):

☐ **Emotional support**: people who will listen and support me (friends, family members):

☐ **Mental health resources**: where to turn if I am struggling with mental health (a good therapist and/or support group in my area, psychiatrist):
  ○ National Maternal Mental Health Hotline (non-emergency, twenty-four seven): 1-833-TLC-MAMA (1-833-852-6262)
  ○ Postpartum Support International Helpline (daytime support and resources): 1-800-944-4773
  ○ National Crisis Hotline (emergency, twenty-four seven): 9-8-8

☐ **Outsourcing**: tasks I would like to outsource or delegate (grocery delivery, house cleaning, laundry service):

☐ **Practical support**: my resources if I need day-to-day help (mother's helper, postpartum doula, night nanny, day nanny):

☐ **Self-care**: manageable things I can do for self-care (showering daily, five minutes of meditation, walking outside):

☐ **Social connection**: how I will remain socially connected and reduce isolation (schedule visits from friends, join a new moms group):

☐ **Relationship care**: here's how my partner and I plan to connect after baby, if applicable (conversations while baby naps, dinners together on Friday nights, get a sitter for a date night):

☐ **Return to work**: my plan for lining up childcare and support for once I return to work, if applicable (day care, nanny, family help, continued outsourcing/delegation of tasks):

RESOURCES

BLACK MOMS

Black Women Do Breastfeed: blackwomendobreastfeed.org

Postpartum Progress Black Mental Health Providers List: postpartumprogress.com/black-mental-health-providers-list

Therapy for Black Girls: therapyforblackgirls.com

BREASTFEEDING/LACTATION SUPPORT

United States Lactation Consultant Association: uslca.org/resources/find-an-ibclc

Kellymom: kellymom.com

La Leche League: lllusa.org

Check with your hospital/birthing center for referrals

INTIMATE PARTNER VIOLENCE/DOMESTIC VIOLENCE

The National Domestic Violence Hotline: 1-800-799-7233

Domestic Shelters: domesticshelters.org

LGBTQ+ FAMILIES

Mombian: mombian.com

National Queer, Trans, and Therapists of Color Network Directory: nqttcn.com/en/mental-health-directory

PFLAG: pflag.org

Postpartum Support International Queer and Trans Support Group: postpartum.net/get-help/queer-parents

LOSS AND GRIEF SUPPORT
Grieve Out Loud: grieveoutloud.org

Postpartum Support International Loss and Grief Support Groups: postpartum.net/get-help/psi-online-support-meetings-2

Share: nationalshare.org/our-programs

The Tears Foundation: thetearsfoundation.org

MEDICATION DURING PREGNANCY AND BREASTFEEDING
MotherToBaby: mothertobaby.org

MENTAL HEALTH
National Crisis Hotline: call or text 9-8-8

National Maternal Mental Health Hotline (Non-emergency, twenty-four seven): 1-833-TLC-MAMA (1-833-852-6262)

Postpartum Support International Hotline (leave a message and get a response during business hours for support and resources): call 1-800-944-4773 or text "help"

Postpartum Support International: postpartum.net

Postpartum Progress: postpartumprogress.com

Contact your OBGYN/physician/midwife

Finding a Therapist:

Postpartum Support International Provider Directory: psi-directory.com

Psychology Today Find a Therapist Directory: psychology-today.com

OpenPath Psychotherapy Collective (affordable therapy): openpathcollective.org

Therapy for Specific Identities:

Latinx Therapy: latinxtherapy.com

National Queer, Trans, and Therapists of Color Network Directory: nqttcn.com/en/mental-health-directory

Therapy for Black Girls: therapyforblackgirls.com

Postpartum Progress Black Mental Health Providers List: postpartumprogress.com/black-mental-health-providers-list

Support Groups:

Postpartum Support International Online Support Meetings: postpartum.net/get-help/psi-online-support-meetings-2/

Check with your hospital/birthing center for groups

Intensive Treatment Options:

Postpartum Support International Intensive Treatment in
the US: postpartum.net/get-help/intensive-perinatal-psych-
treatment-in-the-us/

Mental Health Emergencies:

National Crisis Hotline: call or text 9-8-8

Local Emergency Line: call 9-1-1

Conditions that need emergency help:

- A manic episode (uncharacteristically euphoric, energized, or irritable mood lasting days)
- Postpartum psychosis—bizarre thinking and behavior,
  delusions, hallucinations (see description in chapter eight)
- Feeling like you may *act* on dangerous thoughts, such as
  harming your baby, harming yourself or someone else,
  or abandoning your baby

MENTAL HEALTH FOR DADS

PostpartumDads: postpartumdads.org

PostpartumMen: postpartummen.com

Postpartum Support International Resources for Fathers:
postpartum.net/get-help/resources-for-fathers

PSI monthly chat for dads: postpartum.net/get-help/chat-with-an-expert-for-dads

Parental Mental Health: Factoring in Fathers by Jane I. Honikman and Daniel B. Singley

MILITARY FAMILIES

Postpartum Support International Help for Military Families: postpartum.net/get-help/military-families

Postpartum Support International Military Moms Perinatal Mood Support Group: postpartum.net/get-help/psi-online-support-meetings/#militar--moms

Armed Forces YMCA: asymca.org

Military One Source New Parent Support Program: https: militaryonesource.mil/benefits/new-parent-support-program/

Military Crisis Line: (twenty-four seven) call 9-8-8, press 1 or text 838255

NICU FAMILIES

Hand to Hold: handtohold.org

Postpartum Support International NICU Families Support Group: postpartum.net/get-help/psi-online-support-meetings/#nicu--parents

POSTPARTUM DOULAS

DoulaMatch: doulamatch.net

DONA International: dona.org/what-is-a-doula-2/find-a-doula

RELATIONSHIPS

Gottman Method Couples Therapists: gottmanreferralnetwork.com

Gottman Couples Workshops: https://www.gottman.com/couples/workshops/

Emotionally Focused Therapists (EFT): https://members.iceeft.com/therapist-search/find-an-eft-therapist.php

Bringing Baby Home on demand and live workshops: www.gottman.com/parents

And Baby Makes Three by John Gottman and Julie Schwartz Gottman

The Seven Principles for Making Marriage Work by John Gottman and Nan Silver

Fair Play by Eve Rodsky

SOLO MOMS

Esme: esme.com/resources-for-moms

Single Mothers By Choice: singlemothersbychoice.org

WORKBOOKS

The Pregnancy and Postpartum Mood Workbook by Bethany Warren and Beth Creager Berger

Healing from Reproductive Trauma by Bethany Warren

ACKNOWLEDGMENTS

Family, this book was a team effort! Thank you for giving me time and encouragement for a year of writing. I couldn't have hoped for more support from you three. Bryan, I will never forget how you showed up for me while I wrote this book. Thank you for your time, reading, pep talks, affirmations, and for understanding the importance of this project.

To the Manuscripts LLC team, thank you for a wonderful and butt-kicking program. Kyra Ann Dawkins, Heather Romanowski, and Shanna Heath, I learned so much about writing and marketing from you. A.E. Williams, I appreciate your structural feedback and you seeing value in my book from the beginning. Angela Ivey, you mothered me through the writing process in the best possible way. Michelle Pollack, thank you for holding my hand through social media hesitancy. Christina Sng, you immediately understood where I was trying to go with this book and believed in me the whole way through. Your patience, generosity with your own stories, and humor made editing so lovely. This book is better because of your suggestions. Thank you. For the record, killing cockroaches is not a good form of self-care.

Suzanne, Joy, and Tania, thank you for the gift of your stories. I am inspired by your courage and grateful for these windows into your motherhood experiences that will validate and inform other women.

To the providers who lent their expertise to this book: Bethany Warren, Daniel Singley, Dawn Dickerson, Jen Varela, Kimberly Panganiban, Sheri DeSchaaf, and Victoria Sharma. Each of our conversations was fascinating, and I was floored by how giving you were with your time and your wisdom. Your interviews enriched this book, and I know your information will provide families with help and healing. Jennifer Schere, your interview is not in these chapters, but I'm so grateful for the opportunity to connect with you, and your influence was still important.

Kim, thank you not only for your interview, but also for beta reading and supporting me in everything I do. Your friendship is a rare treasure.

My deepest gratitude to the women who filled out and helped spread the word about the Real-World Motherhood Survey. The responses made me laugh, cry, and nod my head. Your words are activism for new mothers. You brought life to this book, and it wouldn't be the same without you. I hope you enjoy seeing your perspectives in print and shared with the world.

To my clients, who have always inspired and surprised me: thank you for the privilege of being part of your journey.

Beta readers, thank you for devoting time and energy to reading my chapters and giving thoughtful feedback. Each of you offered me something to tuck into this book. Ashlee

Ponder, not only your words but my author mug cheered me on throughout this process. Hayley Graham, Jamie Dredge, and Liz Buron, thank you for your reading, conversations, and texts about this book. I love you and am so lucky to have you by my side in life. Michelle Giering, talking books with you is the best, and it was a privilege to discuss *this* book with you. Letta Page, of course your feedback was helpful and on point, I truly appreciate your time and support. Jenna Keegan, thank you for your important feedback from the perspective of a mom-to-be, and it meant a lot you would do this without even knowing me. Bridget KerMorris, your support has been such a comfort and boost during this process, I'm so grateful for your friendship. Thank you for celebrating me. Tom Waldron, thank you not only for your detailed feedback but for being one of the first people to tell me I was capable of writing, long ago. I'll always be grateful for your presence in my life.

Lauren Niehaus, thank you for beta reading, tracking this process with me, and watching my kids while I wrote this book. Your friendship is so special, and I'm glad we found each other.

Devon DuBois and Alair Olson, thank you for being a constant source of support and a soft place to land. Alair, thank you for your reading and feedback. BB for life.

GS, your mentorship and support in writing this book have been invaluable.

Deanna Moffitt, thank you for helping me see the possibility of having a big goal and for telling me about Book Creators.

Sharyl Page, thank you for being my village, my friend, and my mother-in-law. I love you.

Cindy and Chuck Comfort, thank you for helping me in early motherhood and cheering me on always.

APPENDIX

INTRODUCTION

Budig, Michelle. 2014. *The Fatherhood Bonus and the Motherhood Penalty: Parenthood and the Gender Gap in Pay.* Washington DC: Thirdway.

Douglas, Susan J. 2010. *Enlightened Sexism: The Seductive Message That Feminism's Work Is Done.* New York, NY: Times Books.

Fry, Richard, Carolina Aragao, Kiley Hurst, and Kim Parker. 2023. *In a Growing Share of US Marriages, Husbands and Wives Earn About the Same.* Washington DC: Pew Research Center.

Parker, Kim, Juliana Horowitz, and Renee Stepler. 2017. *On Gender Differences, No Consensus on Nature vs. Nurture.* Washington DC: Pew Research Center.

Wang, Ziyi, Jiaye Liu, Huan Shuai, Zhongxiang Cai, Xia Fu, Yang Liu, Xiong Xiao, Wenhao Zhang, Elise Krabbendam, Shuo Liu, Zhongchun Liu, Zhihui Li, and Bing Xiang Yang. 2021. "Mapping Global Prevalence of Depression Among Postpartum Women." *Translational Psychiatry* 11, no. 543 (October): 1-24. https://doi.org/10.1038/s41398-021-01663-6.

MOTHERHOOD MYTH #1: YOU'RE THE SAME, JUST A MOM

Athan, Aurélie. 2023. Working Definition. Matrescence. Accessed May 28, 2023. https://www.matrescence.com/.

Raphael, Dana. 1973. *The Tender Gift: Breastfeeding.* New York, NY: Schocken Books.

MOTHERHOOD MYTH #2: YOU SHOULD BE BY THE BOOK

Cain Miller, Claire. 2018. "The Relentlessness of Modern Parenting." *The New York Times*, December 25, 2018.

Cain Miller, Claire. 2023. "How Parenting Today is Different, and Harder." *The New York Times*, January 29, 2023.

Hurst, Kiley, Dana Braga, Shannon Greenwood, Chris Baronavski, and Michale Keegan. 2023. "How Today's Parents Say Their Approach to Parenting Does—or Doesn't—Match Their Own Upbringing." *Parenthood* (blog), Pew Research Center. January 24, 2023. https://www.pewresearch.org/social-trends/2023/01/24/how-todays-parents-say-their-approach-to-parenting-does-or-doesnt-match-their-own-upbringing/.

Minkin, Rachel, and Juliana Horowitz. 2023. *Parenting in America Today*. Washington DC: Pew Research Center.

Vyskocilova, Jana, Jan Prasko, Marie Ociskova, Zuzana Sedlackova, and Petr Mozny. 2015. "Values and Values Work in Cognitive Behavioral Therapy." *Activitas Nervosa Superior Rediviva* 57, no. 1-2 (April): 40–48.

https://www.researchgate.net/profile/Marie-Ociskova/publication/298011655_Values_and_values_work_in_cognitive_behavioral_therapy/links/5df480be299bf10bc359a168/Values-and-Values-Work-in-Cognitive-Behavioral-Therapy.pdf.

MOTHERHOOD MYTH #3: IT ALL COMES NATURALLY

Conaboy, Chelsea. 2022. "Maternal Instinct Is a Myth That Men Created." *The New York Times*, August 26, 2022.

Dweck, Carol. 2016. *Mindset: The New Psychology of Success*. New York, NY: Ballantine Books.

Hedgpeth, Dana. 2023. "An Orangutan Struggled to Nurse Her Baby. A Human New Mom Taught Her How." *The Washington Post*, April 1, 2023. https://www.washingtonpost.com/dc-md-va/2023/04/01/new-mom-breastfeed-orangutan-richmond-zoo/.

MOTHERHOOD MYTH #4: THE VILLAGE SHOWS UP

Corrigan, Catherine P., Andrea N. Kwasky, and Carla J. Groh. 2014. "Social Support, Postpartum Depression, and Professional Assistance: A Survey of Mothers in the Midwestern United States." *The Journal of Perinatal Education* 24, no. 1 (January): 48–60. DOI: 10.1891/1058-1243.24.1.48.

Goldberg, Joel. 2016. "It Takes a Village to Determine The Origins of an African Proverb." *Goats and Soda* (blog), NPR. July 30, 2016. https://www.npr.org/sections/goatsandsoda/2016/07/30/487925796/it-takes-a-village-to-determine-the-origins-of-an-african-proverb.

MOTHERHOOD MYTH #5: YOUR BODY BOUNCES RIGHT BACK

Johnson, Sophia K., Jana Pastuschek, Jürgen Rödel, Udo R. Markert, and Tanja Groten. 2018. "Placenta —Worth Trying? Human Maternal Placentophagy: Possible Benefit and Potential Risks." *Geburtshilfe Frauenheilkd* 78, no. 9 (September): 846–852. DOI: 10.1055/a-0674-6275.

The American College of Obstetricians and Gynecologists (ACOG). 2020. "Postpartum Pain Management." The American College of Obstetricians and Gynecologists. Accessed September 1, 2023. https://www.acog.org/womens-health/faqs/postpartum-pain-management.

MOTHERHOOD MYTH #6: SLEEP WHEN THE BABY SLEEPS

Montgomery-Downs, Hawley E., Salvatore P. Insana, Megan M. Clegg-Kraynok, and Laura M. Mancini. 2010. "Normative Longitudinal Maternal Sleep: The First 4 Postpartum Months." *American Journal of Obstetrics and Gynecology* 203, no. 5 (November): 465.e1–7. DOI: 10.1016/j.ajog.2010.06.057.

Pennestri, Marie-Hélène, Christine Laganière, Andrée-Anne Bouvette-Turcot, Irina Pokhvisneva, Meir Steiner, Michael J. Meaney, and Hélène Gaudreau. 2018. "Uninterrupted Infant Sleep, Development, and Maternal Mood." *Pediatrics* 142, no. 6 (December): 1–8. https://doi.org/10.1542/peds.2017-4330.

MOTHERHOOD MYTH #7: YOU CAN HAVE IT ALL

Budig, Michelle. 2014. *The Fatherhood Bonus and The Motherhood Penalty: Parenthood and the Gender Gap in Pay.* Washington DC: Thirdway.

Cain Miller, Claire. 2018. "How Same-Sex Couples Divide Chores, and What It Reveals About Modern Parenting." *The New York Times*, May 16, 2018.

Cain Miller, Claire. 2021. "The Pandemic Created a Child-Care Crisis. Mothers Bore the Burden." *The New York Times*, May 17, 2021.

Coombs, Sarah. 2021. *Paid Leave is Essential for Healthy Moms and Babies.* Washington DC: National Partnership for Women and Families.

Daminger, Allison. 2019. "The Cognitive Dimension of Household Labor." *American Sociological Review* 84, no. 4 (July): 609–633. https://doi.org/10.1177/0003122419859007.

Fry, Richard, Carolina Aragao, Kiley Hurst, and Kim Parker. 2023. *In a Growing Share of US Marriages, Husbands and Wives Earn About the Same.* Washington DC: Pew Research Center.

Organisation for Economic Co-Operation and Development (OECD). 2023. Employment: Time Spent in Paid and Unpaid Work, by Sex. Accessed May 29, 2023. https://stats.oecd.org/index.aspx?queryid=54757.

Parker, Kim, Juliana Horowitz, and Renee Stepler. 2017. *On Gender Differences, No Consensus on Nature vs. Nurture.* Washington DC: Pew Research Center.

Rodsky, Eve. 2019. *Fair Play.* New York, NY: G.P. Putnam's Sons.

Schochet, Leila. 2019. *The Child Care Crisis Is Keeping Women Out of the Workforce.* Washington DC: The Center for American Progress.

MOTHERHOOD MYTH #8: IT'S THE HAPPIEST TIME

American Psychiatric Association. 2013. *Diagnostic and Statistical Manual of Mental Disorders Fifth Edition.* Washington DC: American Psychiatric Association.

Fairbrother, Nichole, Allan H. Young, Patricia Janssen, Martin M. Antony, and Emma Tucker. 2015. "Depression and Anxiety during the Perinatal Period." *BMC Psychiatry* 15, no. 206 (August): 1–9. https://doi.org/10.1186/s12888-015-0526-6.

Frawley, Timothy, and Denise McGuinness. 2023. "Dysphoric Milk Ejection Reflex (D-MER) and its Implications for Mental Health Nursing." *International Journal of Mental Health Nursing* 32, no. 2 (January): 620–626. https://doi.org/10.1111/inm.13115.

Guintivano, Jerry, Tracy Mauck, and Samantha Meltzer-Brody. 2018. "Predictors of Postpartum Depression: A Comprehensive Review of the Last Decade of Evidence." *Clinical Obstetrics and Gynecology* 61, no. 3 (September): 591–603. https://doi.org/10.1097/GRF.0000000000000368.

Klaman, Stacey, and Kea Turner. 2016. "Prevalence of Perinatal Depression in the Military: A Systematic Review of the Literature." *Maternal and Child Health Journal* 20 (August): 52–65. DOI: 10.1007/s10995-016-2172-0.

Masters, Grace A., Julie Hugunin, Lulu Xu, Christine M. Ulbricht, Tiffany A. Moore Simas, Jean Y. Ko, and Nancy Byatt. 2022. "Prevalence of Bipolar Disorder in Perinatal Women: A Systematic Review and Meta-Analysis." *The Journal of Clinical Psychiatry* 83, no. 5 (July): e1–e11. DOI: 10.4088/JCP.21r14045.

Mukherjee, Soumyadeep, Mary Jo Trepka, Dudith Pierre-Victor, Raed Bahelah, and Tenesha Avent. 2016. "Racial/Ethnic Disparities in Antenatal Depression in the United States: A Systemic Review." *Maternal and Child Health Journal* 20 (March): 1780–1797. https://doi.org/10.1007/s10995-016-1989-x.

Postpartum Support International. 2015. *Perinatal Mood and Anxiety Disorders Fact Sheet.* Portland, OR: Postpartum Support International.

Scarff, Jonathan R. 2019. "Postpartum Depression in Men." *Innovations in Clinical Neuroscience* 16, no. 5-6 (May-June): 11–14. https://www.ncbi.nlm.nih.gov/pmc/articles/PMC6659987/.

Sit, Dorothy, Anthony J. Rothschild, and Katherine L. Wisner. 2006. "A Review of Postpartum Psychosis." *Journal of Women's Health* 15, no. 4 (May): 352–368. DOI: 10.1089/jwh.2006.15.352.

VanderKruik, Rachel, Maria Barriex, Doris Chou, Tomas Allen, Lale Say, and Lee S. Cohen. 2017. "The Global Prevalence of Postpartum Psychosis: A Systematic Review." *BMC Psychiatry* 17, no. 272 (July): 1–9. https://doi.org/10.1186/s12888-017-1427-7.

Van Niel, Maureen Sayres, and Jennifer L. Payne. 2020. "Perinatal Depression: A Review." *Cleveland Clinic Journal of Medicine* 87, no. 5 (May): 273–277. https://doi.org/10.3949/ccjm.87a.19054.

Vladan, Starcevic, Guy D. Eslick, Kirupamani Viswasam, and David Berle. 2020. "Symptoms of Obsessive-Compulsive Disorder During Pregnancy and the Postpartum Period: A Systematic Review and Meta-Analysis." *Psychiatric Quarterly* 91 (May): 965–981. https://doi.org/10.1007/s11126-020-09769-8.

Wesseloo, Richard, Astrid M. Kamperman, Trine Munk-Olsen, Victor J.M. Pop, Steven A. Kushner, and Veerle Berghink. 2016. "Risk of Postpartum Relapse in Bipolar Disorder and Postpartum Psychosis: A Systematic Review and Meta-Analysis." *American Journal of Psychiatry* 173, no. 2 (February): 117–127. DOI: 10.1176/appi.ajp.2015.15010124.

Yildiz, Pelin Dikmen, Susan Ayers, and Louise Phillips. 2017. "The Prevalence of Posttraumatic Stress Disorder in Pregnancy and After Birth: A Systematic Review and Meta-Analysis." *Journal of Affective Disorders* 208 (January): 634-645. https://doi.org/10.1016/j.jad.2016.10.009.

MOTHERHOOD MYTH #9: GOOD MOMS DON'T HAVE BAD THOUGHTS

Law, Naomi K., Pauline L. Hall, and Anna Cheshire. 2021. "Common Negative Thoughts in Early Motherhood and Their Relationship to Guilt, Shame, and Depression." *Journal of Child and Family Studies* 30 (June): 1831–1845. https://doi.org/10.1007/s10826-021-01968-6.

Neff, Kristin. 2023. "What is Self-Compassion?" Self-Compassion. https://self-compassion.org/the-three-elements-of-self-compassion-2/.

Zhang, Dexing, Eric K. P. Lee, Eva C. W. Mak, C. Y. Ho, Samuel Y. S. Wong. 2021. "Mindfulness-Based Interventions: An Overall Review." *British Medical Bulletin* 138, no. 1 (June): 41–57. https://doi.org/10.1093/bmb/ldab005.

MOTHERHOOD MYTH #10: A BABY BRINGS YOU CLOSER TOGETHER

Gottman, John M., and Julie Schwartz Gottman. 2007. *And Baby Makes Three.* New York, NY: Crown Publishers.

Rodsky, Eve. 2019. *Fair Play.* New York, NY: G.P. Putnam's Sons.